Super Easy and Quick Mediterranean Diet Cookbook for Beginners

© **Copyright 2024 – All rights reserved.**

The content contained within this book may not be reproduced, duplicated, or transmitted without direct written permission from the author or the publisher.

Under no circumstances will any blame or legal responsibility be held against the publisher or author for any damages, reparation, or monetary loss due to the information contained within this book, either directly or indirectly.

Legal Notice:

This book is copyright-protected. It is only for personal use. You cannot amend, distribute, sell, use, quote, or paraphrase any part of the content within this book without the consent of the author or publisher.

Disclaimer Notice:

Please note that information contained within this document is for educational and entertainment purposes only. All efforts have been executed to present accurate, up-to-date, reliable, and complete information. No warranties of any kind are declared or implied. Readers acknowledge that the author is not engaged in the rendering of legal, financial, medical, or professional advice. The content within this book has been derived from various sources. Please consult a licensed professional before attempting any techniques outlined in this book.

By reading this document, the reader agrees that under no circumstances is the author responsible for any losses, direct or indirect, that are incurred as a result of the use of the information contained within this document, including, but not limited to, errors, omissions, or inaccuracies.

TABLE OF CONTENT

INTRODUCTION 11

MEZE, ANTIPASTI, TAPAS 12

    Tzatziki 13

    Baba Ganoush 14

    Zhoug Sauce 15

    Zucchini Dip 16

    Mediterranean Artichoke Dip 17

    Eggplant Rollatini 18

    Mediterranean Veggie Platter 19

    Mediterranean Stuffed Mini Bell Peppers 20

    Hummus Plate 21

    Stuffed Grape Leaves (Dolmas) 22

    Mediterranean Caprese Skewers 23

    Sardine and Herb Bruschetta 24

    Kalamata Olive Tapenade 25

    Chunky Red Pepper and Feta Dip 26

    Mediterranean Mini Spinach Quiche 27

BEEF & LAMB RECIPES 28

    Beef Kebabs 29

    Greek Style Grilled Lamb Chops 30

    Stewed Beef in Tomato Sauce 31

    Lamb Meatballs 32

    Tender Lamb Shanks 33

    Pulled Lamb Shoulder 34

    Beef and Prunes 35

    Ground Beef Stir Fry 37

    Mediterranean Steak Bites 38

Steak Bowls..39

Beef Cacciatore...40

Moussaka 42

Lamb Souvlaki..44

Bifteki (Greek Beef Patties)...45

Greek-Style Beef Stuffed Portobello Mushrooms 46

POULTRY 48

Mediterranean Grilled Chicken...49

Stuffed Chicken Breast..50

Balsamic Glazed Chicken Thighs...51

Turkey Meatballs 52

Greek Style Lemon 53

Chicken Skewers 53

Mediterranean Turkey Stuffed Bell Peppers..54

Spanish-Style Chicken Casserole..55

Chicken Skillet..57

Chicken Piccata..58

Mediterranean Turkey Bowls 59

Zucchini Stuffed with Turkey 60

Turkey Meatball and Orzo Bowl 62

Couscous & Chicken Bake..64

Baked Chicken Thighs in Yogurt Sauce with Herbs..............................65

Mediterranean Turkey Meatloaf 66

Turkey Wraps...67

Turkey Panini 68

Turkey Pieces Baked in Pumpkin 69

Duck Breast with Figs and Olives...70

Xinomavro Duck with 71

Cornmeal Cream..71

Duck Breast with 73

Honey and Spices.. 73

SEAFOOD & FISH.. 75

Grilled Mediterranean Salmon 76

Mediterranean Baked Cod 77

Lemon Garlic Shrimp Skewers 78

Mediterranean Style Seared Tuna 79

Baked Mediterranean.. 80

Stuffed Sole.. 80

Grilled Lemon Garlic Scallops 81

Mediterranean Style Baked 82

Red Snapper 82

Shrimp and Vegetable Stir-Fry... 83

Lemon Herb Baked 84

Salmon Patties... 84

Mediterranean Style 85

Steamed Mussels.. 85

Salmon with White Sauce 86

Clams Toscano.. 87

Greek Stuffed Squid 88

Calamari Stew 90

Octopus Braised in Red Wine 91

Octopus in Honey Sauce 92

Mahi-Mahi and Mushrooms 93

Shrimp and Feta Saganaki 94

Herb-Crumbed Fish Saganaki 95

Mediterranean Fish Kebabs 96

HEALTHY VEGETARIAN & VEGAN RECIPES 97
- *Zucchini Noodles with Pesto 98*
- *Mushroom and Spinach Stuffed Portobello Mushrooms...........................99*
- *Cauliflower Rice Bowl 100*
- *Vegetable Ratatouille 101*
- *Mediterranean Veggie Stir-Fry 102*
- *Spaghetti Squash with Tomato Basil Sauce..103*
- *Eggplant Caponata 105*
- *Cauliflower and Chickpea Curry..106*
- *Balsamic Roasted Green Beans 107*
- *Sautéed Kale..108*
- *Green Bean Stew 109*
- *Mediterranean Gnocchi...110*
- *Vegetarian Chili...111*
- *Turkish Beet Greens..112*
- *Zucchini and Tomato Casserole 113*
- *Roasted Brussels Sprouts and Pecans..114*
- *Briami 115*
- *Fasolakia..116*
- *Stuffed Eggplant with Onion and Tomato..117*
- *Stuffed Eggplant 119*
- *with Couscous and Pecans..119*

SOUPS 121
- *Vegetable Soup..122*
- *Lentil and Spinach Soup..123*
- *Greek Lemon Chicken 124*
- *Soup (Avgolemono) 124*
- *Tuscan White Bean Soup...125*
- *Chunky Mediterranean..126*

Tomato Soup 126

Chicken, Chickpea & Zucchini Soup 127

Chicken & Kale Soup 128

Chicken & Bok Choy Soup with Ginger & Mushrooms 129

Rainbow Minestrone 130

Bean & Barley Soup 131

RICE, GRAIN, PASTA, COUSCOUS 132

Mediterranean Kale Fried Rice 133

Mediterranean Tomato Rice 134

Mediterranean Pasta Salad 135

Brown Rice Pilaf 136

Mediterranean Style 138

Spaghetti Squash 138

Pasta Primavera 139

Lemon Garlic Chickpea Pasta 140

Fakorizo 141

Spanakorizo 142

Rotini with Spinach, Cherry 143

Tomatoes, and Feta 143

Puglia-Style Pasta with 144

Broccoli Sauce 144

Orzo with Feta and 145

Marinated Peppers 145

Mediterranean Grain Tabbouleh 146

Pesto Chicken Quinoa Bowls 147

Winter Squash and 148

Greens Couscous 148

Couscous Stuffed Bell Peppers 150

Grilled Vegetable Couscous Bowl 151

Mediterranean Couscous Soup 152

Mediterranean Couscous Skillet 153

Greek Couscous Patties 154

SIDE DISHES 155

Couscous with Eggplant and 156

Tomatoes 156

Bulgur with Eggplant, Zucchini, Tomatoes, and Mushrooms 157

Brown Rice with 158

Zucchini and Spinach 158

Couscous with Zucchini, Green Peas, and Sweet Peppers 159

Couscous with 160

Vegetables and Cheese 160

Quinoa with Spinach in 161

Creamy Sauce 161

Spinach Casserole with 163

Two Types of Cheese 163

Warm Salad with 164

Quinoa and Vegetables 164

Bulgur and Quinoa 166

Porridge with Onions 166

Bulgur and Orzo 167

Pasta with Vegetables 167

SALAD 168

Quinoa Tabbouleh Salad 169

Mediterranean Zoodle Salad 170

Shrimp and Avocado Salad 171

Mediterranean Chickpea 172

and Quinoa Salad 172

Green Mediterranean Salad 173

Beet and Walnut Salad *174*

Cabbage and Carrot Salad *175*

Watermelon and Feta Salad *176*

Horta (Warm Greens Salad) *177*

Zucchini and Ricotta Salad *178*

Sicilian Salad *179*

Citrus Avocado Salad *180*

Italian Summer Vegetable *181*

Barley Salad *181*

Greek Chicken Gyro Salad *182*

Cauliflower and Farro Salad *183*

DESSERTS **184**

Mediterranean Fruit Sorbet *185*

Italian Chocolate Coffee Cake *186*

Greek Almond Cookies *187*

Baked Pears with *188*

Ricotta and Honey *188*

Fruit Skewers with Yogurt Dip *189*

Greek Yogurt Bark with Berries *190*

Greek Orange Honey *191*

Cake with Pistachios *191*

Italian Tiramisu *192*

Greek Baklava *194*

Cherry Clafoutis *196*

BREADS, FLATBREADS, PIZZA'S **197**

Greek Salad Pita Pockets *198*

Mediterranean Flatbread Pizza *199*

Veggie Pizza *200*

Mediterranean Flatbread *201*

Mediterranean Olive Bread 203

Banana Walnut Bread 204

Mediterranean Pide 205

COCKTAIL'S, DRINKS **207**

Mediterranean-Style 208

Mint Lemonade 208

Mediterranean Ginger-Rosemary Drink 209

Spiced Pomegranate Ginger 210

Beer Mocktail 210

Honey Mint Green Iced Tea 211

Carrot Ginger Juice 212

Greek Yogurt and Berry Smoothie 213

Mango and Spinach Smoothie 214

28-DAY MEAL PLAN **215**

CONCLUSION **220**

INTRODUCTION

Embrace a Healthier, Tastier Lifestyle with the Mediterranean Diet

Are you ready to start living a healthier lifestyle and leave behind those bad eating habits? Do you dream of losing weight without sacrificing your love for food? If your answer is yes, then you're in the right place. You are about to embark on a journey that will revolutionize your eating habits and improve your health in every aspect.

Long lauded for its extraordinary health advantages, the Mediterranean diet is more than simply food. It is a way of life. Best known for its positive impact on heart health, weight management, and energy levels, this way of eating is as delicious as it is nutritious. And now, with our carefully crafted Beginner Cookbook, you can experience these benefits firsthand. Inside these pages, you'll discover 170 simple yet mouth-watering dishes that make healthy eating both enjoyable and accessible. From savory meats and seafood to vibrant vegetables and satisfying grains, this cookbook offers a wide variety of recipes to suit everyone's taste. Whether you're a seasoned chef or a complete beginner, our simple instructions will guide you through the process of creating wholesome meals that your family will love.

This book is more than just a collection of recipes. We've included detailed nutrition facts for each meal, providing you with the necessary knowledge to make informed decisions about what you're putting on your plate. Understanding the nutritional value of your food is the first step toward a healthier lifestyle, and with this cookbook, you'll embark on your culinary journey with confidence.

So why wait? The Mediterranean diet is your gateway to a healthier, happier you. With this cookbook, you'll not only enjoy the rich, diverse flavors of the Mediterranean but also reap the long-term benefits that come with it.

Taking control of your health without giving up the joy of a delicious meal is easier than you think. Seize this opportunity to transform your diet and your life—one recipe at a time.

MEZE, ANTIPASTI, TAPAS

Tzatziki

Prep time: 10 min | Cook time: 30 min | Serving: 6

INGREDIENTS

- *1 cup Greek yogurt*
- *1/2 cucumber, grated and squeezed to remove excess moisture*
- *2 cloves garlic, minced*
- *1 tablespoon extra-virgin olive oil*
- *1 tablespoon fresh lemon juice*
- *1 tablespoon chopped fresh dill (or 1 teaspoon dried dill)*
- *Salt and black pepper, to taste*
- *Optional garnish: chopped fresh parsley, a drizzle of olive oil*

1) In a mixing bowl, combine Greek yogurt, grated cucumber, minced garlic, olive oil, lemon juice, and chopped dill.
2) Season with salt and black pepper to taste. Stir until well combined.
3) Cover the bowl and refrigerate for at least 30 minutes to allow the flavors to meld together.
4) Before serving, taste the tzatziki and adjust seasoning if needed.
5) Transfer the tzatziki to a serving bowl.
6) If desired, garnish with chopped fresh parsley and a drizzle of olive oil.
7) Serve the Mediterranean Diet Tzatziki as a dip with fresh vegetables, pita bread, or as a sauce for grilled meats and fish.

NUTRITION

Cal 60; Fat 4 g; Carb 5 g;
Protein 2 g; Fiber: 1 g; Sodium: 80 mg

Baba Ganoush

| Prep time: 10 min | Cook time: 40 min | Serving: 6 |

INGREDIENTS

- *2 medium eggplants*
- *2 cloves garlic, minced*
- *2 tablespoons tahini*
- *2 tablespoons lemon juice*
- *2 tablespoons extra-virgin olive oil, plus more for drizzling*
- *Salt, to taste*
- *Black pepper, to taste*
- *Optional garnish: chopped fresh parsley, paprika, pine nuts*

1) Preheat the oven to 400°F (200°C).
2) Using a fork, prick the eggplants in several places. Place them on a baking sheet lined with parchment paper.
3) Roast the eggplants in the preheated oven for 30-40 minutes, or until they are very soft and collapsed. Remove from the oven and let cool.
4) Once the eggplants are cool enough to handle, slice them open and scoop out the flesh into a bowl, discarding the skins.
5) Mash the eggplant flesh with a fork or potato masher until smooth.
6) Add minced garlic, tahini, lemon juice, and olive oil to the mashed eggplant. Stir until well combined.
7) Season the Baba Ganoush with salt and black pepper to taste.
8) Transfer the Baba Ganoush to a serving bowl. Drizzle with extra-virgin olive oil and sprinkle with chopped fresh parsley, paprika, or pine nuts if desired.
9) Serve the Baba Ganoush with pita bread, crackers, or fresh vegetables for dipping.

NUTRITION

Cal 120; Fat 10 g; Carb 8 g;
Protein 2 g; Fiber: 3 g; Sodium: 15 mg

Zhoug Sauce

| Prep time: 10 min | Cook time 0 min | Serving: 8 |

INGREDIENTS

- *1 cup fresh cilantro leaves, packed*
- *1 cup fresh parsley leaves, packed*
- *2 cloves garlic*
- *1 small jalapeño pepper, seeds removed (adjust to taste for spiciness)*
- *1 teaspoon ground cumin*
- *1/2 teaspoon ground coriander*
- *1/4 teaspoon red pepper flakes*
- *1/4 cup extra-virgin olive oil*
- *1 tablespoon fresh lemon juice*
- *Salt, to taste*

1) In a food processor or blender, combine cilantro leaves, parsley leaves, garlic, jalapeño pepper, ground cumin, ground coriander, and red pepper flakes.
2) Pulse the ingredients until coarsely chopped.
3) With the food processor running, slowly drizzle in the extra-virgin olive oil and lemon juice until the mixture is smooth and well combined. You may need to scrape down the sides of the bowl with a spatula as needed.
4) Taste the Zhoug Sauce and season with salt to taste. Adjust the spiciness by adding more jalapeño if desired.
5) Transfer the Zhoug Sauce to a jar or airtight container.
6) Store the sauce in the refrigerator for up to one week.
7) Serve the Zhoug Sauce as a condiment for grilled meats, roasted vegetables, falafel, or as a spread on sandwiches and wraps.

NUTRITION

Cal 30; Fat 2 g; Carb 3 g;
Protein 1 g; Fiber: 1 g; Sodium: 160 mg

Zucchini Dip

Prep time: 10 min | Cook time: 20 min | Serving: 6

INGREDIENTS

- *2 medium zucchinis, grated*
- *2 cloves garlic, minced*
- *2 tablespoons extra-virgin olive oil*
- *1 tablespoon lemon juice*
- *1/4 cup Greek yogurt*
- *1 tablespoon chopped fresh dill*
- *Salt, to taste*
- *Black pepper, to taste*
- *Optional garnish: drizzle of olive oil, sprinkle of paprika, chopped fresh parsley*

1) Preheat the oven to 400°F (200°C).
2) Place the grated zucchini in a clean kitchen towel and squeeze out excess moisture.
3) In a mixing bowl, combine the grated zucchini, minced garlic, extra-virgin olive oil, lemon juice, Greek yogurt, and chopped fresh dill.
4) Season with salt and black pepper to taste. Stir until well combined.
5) Transfer the mixture to a baking dish and spread it out evenly.
6) Bake in the preheated oven for 15-20 minutes or until the dip is heated through and the top is lightly golden.
7) Remove from the oven and let the dip cool slightly before serving.
8) If desired, garnish the Mediterranean Zucchini Dip with a drizzle of olive oil, a sprinkle of paprika, and chopped fresh parsley.
9) Serve the dip warm or at room temperature with pita bread, crackers, or fresh vegetables for dipping.

NUTRITION

Cal 70; Fat 5 g; Carb 6 g;
Protein 2 g; Fiber: 2 g; Sodium: 150 mg

Mediterranean Artichoke Dip

Prep time: 10 min	Cook time 25 min	Serving: 6

INGREDIENTS

- *1 can (14 ounces) artichoke hearts, drained and chopped*
- *1 cup grated Parmesan cheese*
- *1/2 cup Greek yogurt*
- *1/4 cup mayonnaise*
- *2 cloves garlic, minced*
- *1 tablespoon fresh lemon juice*
- *1 tablespoon chopped fresh parsley*
- *1/2 teaspoon dried oregano*
- *Salt, to taste*
- *Black pepper, to taste*
- *Optional garnish: chopped fresh parsley, red pepper flakes*

1) Preheat the oven to 375°F (190°C).
2) In a mixing bowl, combine the chopped artichoke hearts, grated Parmesan cheese, Greek yogurt, mayonnaise, minced garlic, lemon juice, chopped fresh parsley, and dried oregano.
3) Season with salt and black pepper to taste. Stir until well combined.
4) Transfer the mixture to an oven-safe baking dish and spread it out evenly.
5) Bake in the preheated oven for 20-25 minutes or until the dip is bubbly and the top is lightly golden.
6) Remove from the oven and let the dip cool slightly before serving.
7) If desired, garnish the Mediterranean Artichoke Dip with chopped fresh parsley and a sprinkle of red pepper flakes for some extra heat.
8) Serve the dip warm with pita bread, crackers, or fresh vegetables for dipping.

NUTRITION

Cal 130; Fat 10 g; Carb 7 g;
Protein 4 g; Fiber: 2 g; Sodium: 260 mg

Eggplant Rollatini

| Prep time: 15 min | Cook time 30 min | Serving: 2 |

INGREDIENTS

- *1 large eggplant, thinly sliced lengthwise*
- *Olive oil for brushing*
- *1 cup ricotta cheese*
- *1 cup chopped spinach*
- *2 cloves garlic, minced*
- *1/4 cup grated Parmesan cheese*
- *1 tablespoon chopped fresh basil*
- *Salt and black pepper, to taste*
- *1 cup marinara sauce*
- *Fresh parsley, chopped for garnish (optional)*

1) Preheat your oven to 375°F (190°C).
2) Place the thinly sliced eggplant on a baking sheet lined with parchment paper. Brush both sides of the eggplant slices with olive oil.
3) Grill the eggplant slices on a preheated grill or bake them in the preheated oven for 5-7 minutes on each side or until tender. Remove from heat and let them cool slightly.
4) In a mixing bowl, combine the ricotta cheese, chopped spinach, minced garlic, grated Parmesan cheese, chopped fresh basil, salt, and black pepper. Stir until well combined.
5) Spread a spoonful of the ricotta mixture onto each eggplant slice, then roll them up tightly.
6) Place the rolled eggplant slices seam-side down in a baking dish.
7) Pour marinara sauce over the top of the rolled eggplant slices, covering them evenly.
8) Bake in the preheated oven for 20-25 minutes or until heated through and the sauce is bubbly.
9) Remove from the oven and let them cool for a few minutes.

NUTRITION

Cal 350; Fat 20 g; Carb 25 g;
Protein 20 g; Fiber: 10 g; Sodium: 680 mg

Mediterranean Veggie Platter

| | Prep time: 10 min | | Cook time 0 min | | Serving: 2 |

INGREDIENTS

- *1 cucumber, sliced*
- *1 cup cherry tomatoes*
- *1 bell pepper, thinly sliced*
- *1 carrot, cut into sticks*
- *1/2 cup olives (assorted varieties)*
- *1/2 cup hummus for dipping*

1) Arrange the sliced cucumber, cherry tomatoes, bell pepper strips, carrot sticks, and olives on a large serving platter.

2) Place a bowl of hummus in the center of the platter for dipping.

3) Serve the Mediterranean Veggie Platter immediately as a healthy and refreshing appetizer or snack.

NUTRITION

Cal 150; Fat 8 g; Carb 18 g;
Protein 6 g; Fiber: 7 g; Sodium: 400 mg

Mediterranean Stuffed Mini Bell Peppers

| Prep time: 15 min | Cook time 0 min | Serving: 2 |

INGREDIENTS

- *6 mini bell peppers, halved and seeds removed*
- *1/2 cup whipped feta cheese*
- *1/4 cup diced cucumber*
- *1/4 cup cherry tomatoes, quartered*
- *2 tablespoons sliced olives*
- *1 tablespoon chopped fresh herbs (such as parsley, basil, or dill)*
- *Olive oil for drizzling (optional)*
- *Balsamic glaze for drizzling (optional)*

1) In a mixing bowl, combine the whipped feta cheese, diced cucumber, quartered cherry tomatoes, sliced olives, and chopped fresh herbs. Mix until well combined.

2) Spoon the Mediterranean filling into each halved mini bell pepper, dis-tributing it evenly among them.

3) Arrange the stuffed mini bell peppers on a serving platter.

4) If desired, drizzle olive oil and balsamic glaze over the stuffed peppers for added flavor and presentation.

5) Serve the Mediterranean Stuffed Mini Bell Peppers immediately as a colorful and flavorful appetizer or snack.

NUTRITION

Cal 120; Fat 9 g; Carb 7 g;
Protein 4 g; Fiber: 2 g; Sodium: 280 mg

Hummus Plate

Prep time: 10 min | Cook time: 0 min | Serving: 2

INGREDIENTS

- *1 cup hummus*
- *1/2 cup diced tomatoes*
- *1/2 cup cucumber slices*
- *1/4 cup olives (assorted varieties)*
- *1/4 cup crumbled feta cheese*
- *1 tablespoon olive oil for drizzling*
- *Whole-grain crackers or vegetable sticks, for serving*

1) Spread the hummus evenly onto a large serving plate, creating a smooth base.

2) Arrange the diced tomatoes, cucumber slices, olives, and crumbled feta cheese on top of the hummus, distributing them evenly across the plate.

3) Drizzle olive oil over the toppings for added flavor and presentation.

4) Serve the Mediterranean Hummus Plate immediately with whole-grain crackers or vegetable sticks for dipping.

NUTRITION

Cal 300; Fat 20 g; Carb 25 g; Protein 10 g; Fiber: 8 g; Sodium: 600 mg

Stuffed Grape Leaves (Dolmas)

Prep time: 30 min	Cook time 120 min	Serving: 2

INGREDIENTS

- *10-12 grape leaves, rinsed, and drained (if using jarred, rinse well to remove excess brine)*
- *1/2 cup cooked rice*
- *2 tablespoons pine nuts, toasted*
- *2 tablespoons currants or raisins*
- *1 tablespoon fresh lemon juice*
- *1 tablespoon chopped fresh herbs (such as parsley, dill, and mint)*
- *1 tablespoon olive oil, plus extra for drizzling*
- *Salt and black pepper, to taste*
- *Greek yogurt for serving (optional)*

1) In a mixing bowl, combine the cooked rice, toasted pine nuts, currants or raisins, fresh lemon juice, chopped fresh herbs, and olive oil. Season with salt and black pepper to taste. Mix well to combine.
2) Lay a grape leaf flat on a clean work surface, vein side up. Place a small spoonful of the rice mixture near the stem end of the leaf.
3) Fold the bottom of the leaf over the filling, then fold in the sides, and roll up tightly into a cylinder shape. Repeat with the remaining grape leaves and filling.
4) Place the stuffed grape leaves seam side down in a saucepan or skillet, arranging them snugly in a single layer.
5) Drizzle a little olive oil over the stuffed grape leaves, then pour enough water into the pan to just cover them.
6) Place a heatproof plate or lid directly on top of the stuffed grape leaves to keep them submerged in the liquid.
7) Bring the water to a gentle simmer over medium heat. Cover the pan and cook the stuffed grape leaves for 30 minutes or until the rice is tender.
8) Remove the stuffed grape leaves from the pan and let them cool to room temperature.
9) Once cooled, transfer the stuffed grape leaves to a serving platter and refrigerate for at least 2 hours to chill before serving.
10) Serve the Stuffed Grape Leaves (Dolmas) chilled as a refreshing ap-petizer, accompanied by Greek yogurt for dipping, if desired.

NUTRITION
Cal 200; Fat 8 g; Carb 30 g;
Protein 3 g; Fiber: 2 g; Sodium: 450 mg

Mediterranean Caprese Skewers

| Prep time: 10 min | Cook time 0 min | Serving: 2 |

INGREDIENTS

- *12 cherry tomatoes*
- *12 mini mozzarella balls (bocconcini)*
- *12 fresh basil leaves*
- *Balsamic glaze for drizzling*
- *Sea salt for sprinkling*

1) Thread one cherry tomato, one mini mozzarella ball, and one fresh basil leaf onto each skewer repeating until all ingredients are used.

2) Arrange the Mediterranean Caprese Skewers on a serving platter or plate.

3) Drizzle balsamic glaze over the skewers, ensuring each one is lightly coated.

4) Sprinkle a pinch of sea salt over the skewers for added flavor.

5) Serve the Mediterranean Caprese Skewers immediately as a delightful and refreshing appetizer or snack.

NUTRITION

Cal 150; Fat 9 g; Carb 7 g; Protein 8 g; Fiber: 2 g; Sodium: 300 mg

Sardine and Herb Bruschetta

Prep time: 10 min | Cook time: 5 min | Serving: 4

INGREDIENTS

- *1 can (4.4 ounces) sardines in olive oil, drained*
- *4 slices of whole-grain bread*
- *2 tablespoons extra-virgin olive oil*
- *1 clove garlic, peeled and halved*
- *1 tablespoon chopped fresh parsley*
- *1 tablespoon chopped fresh basil*
- *1 tablespoon chopped fresh chives*
- *1 teaspoon lemon zest*
- *Salt, to taste*
- *Black pepper, to taste*
- *Optional garnish: lemon wedges, extra herbs for topping*

1) Preheat the broiler on your oven.
2) Brush both sides of the whole-grain bread slices with extra-virgin olive oil.
3) Place the bread slices on a baking sheet and broil for 1-2 minutes on each side or until golden brown and crispy. Watch closely to prevent burning.
4) Remove the toasted bread from the oven and rub one side of each slice with the cut side of the halved garlic clove.
5) In a small bowl, mash the drained sardines with a fork.
6) In another bowl, combine chopped fresh parsley, basil, chives, and lemon zest.
7) Spread the mashed sardines evenly onto the garlic-rubbed side of each toasted bread slice.
8) Sprinkle the herb mixture over the sardines.
9) Season with salt and black pepper to taste.
10) If desired, garnish with lemon wedges and extra chopped herbs.

NUTRITION

Cal 180; Fat 8 g; Carb 18 g;
Protein 10 g; Fiber: 2 g; Sodium: 280 mg

Kalamata Olive Tapenade

Prep time: 10 min	Cook time 0 min	Serving: 1 cup

INGREDIENTS

- *1 cup pitted Kalamata olives*
- *2 cloves garlic*
- *2 tablespoons capers, drained*
- *2 anchovy fillets (optional)*
- *2 tablespoons fresh lemon juice*
- *2 tablespoons extra-virgin olive oil*
- *1 tablespoon chopped fresh parsley*
- *1 teaspoon Dijon mustard*
- *Black pepper, to taste*

1) In a food processor, combine the pitted Kalamata olives, garlic cloves, capers, and anchovy fillets (if using).
2) Pulse the ingredients until coarsely chopped.
3) Add fresh lemon juice, extra-virgin olive oil, chopped fresh parsley, and Dijon mustard to the food processor.
4) Pulse again until the mixture is finely chopped and well combined. You can adjust the texture according to your preference.
5) Taste the tapenade and season with black pepper to taste. Depending on the saltiness of your olives and capers, additional salt may not be needed.
6) Transfer the tapenade to a serving bowl or jar.
7) Serve the Kalamata Olive Tapenade as a spread on crusty bread, crackers, or as a condiment for sandwiches, wraps, or grilled meats.

NUTRITION

Cal 70; Fat 7 g; Carb 2 g;
Protein 1 g; Fiber: 1 g; Sodium: 320 mg

Chunky Red Pepper and Feta Dip

| Prep time: 10 min | Cook time 0 min | Serving: 6 |

INGREDIENTS

- *1 large red bell pepper, roasted, peeled, and diced*
- *1/2 cup crumbled feta cheese*
- *1/4 cup Greek yogurt*
- *2 tablespoons extra-virgin olive oil*
- *1 clove garlic, minced*
- *1 tablespoon fresh lemon juice*
- *1 tablespoon chopped fresh parsley*
- *Salt, to taste*
- *Black pepper, to taste*
- *Optional garnish: chopped fresh parsley, drizzle of olive oil*

1) If you haven't already, roast the red bell pepper by placing it directly over a gas flame or under a broiler until charred on all sides. Then, place it in a bowl covered with plastic wrap for a few minutes to steam. Once cooled, peel off the charred skin, remove the seeds, and dice the pepper.
2) In a mixing bowl, combine the diced roasted red bell pepper, crumbled feta cheese, Greek yogurt, extra-virgin olive oil, minced garlic, fresh lemon juice, and chopped fresh parsley.
3) Season with salt and black pepper to taste. Stir until all ingredients are well combined.
4) Taste and adjust seasoning if necessary.
5) Transfer the Chunky Red Pepper and Feta Dip to a serving bowl.
6) If desired, garnish with chopped fresh parsley and a drizzle of olive oil.
7) Serve the dip with pita bread, crackers, or fresh vegetables for dipping.

NUTRITION
Cal 90; Fat 7 g; Carb 4 g;
Protein 3 g; Fiber: 1 g; Sodium: 180 mg

Mediterranean Mini Spinach Quiche

| Prep time: 15 min | Cook time 25 min | Serving: 6 |

INGREDIENTS

- *1 package (10 ounces) frozen chopped spinach, thawed and drained*
- *3/4 cup crumbled feta cheese*
- *1/3 cup chopped sun-dried tomatoes*
- *3 green onions, thinly sliced*
- *6 large eggs*
- *3/4 cup milk (you can use whole milk, low-fat milk, or plant-based milk)*
- *1/2 teaspoon dried oregano*
- *Salt and black pepper, to taste*
- *Cooking spray or olive oil for greasing the muffin tin*

1) Preheat your oven to 375°F (190°C). Grease a 12-cup muffin tin with cooking spray or olive oil.
2) In a mixing bowl, combine the thawed and drained chopped spinach, crumbled feta cheese, chopped sun-dried tomatoes, and sliced green on-ions. Mix well.
3) In a separate bowl, whisk together the eggs, milk, dried oregano, salt, and black pepper until well combined.
4) Pour the egg mixture over the spinach mixture and stir until everything is evenly coated.
5) Divide the mixture evenly among the prepared muffin cups, filling each cup almost to the top.
6) Bake in the preheated oven for about 20-25 minutes or until the mini quiches are set and the tops are lightly golden brown.
7) Remove from the oven and let the quiches cool in the muffin tin for a few minutes.
8) Carefully remove the mini quiches from the muffin tin and transfer them to a wire rack to cool slightly before serving.
9) Serve the Mediterranean Mini Spinach Quiche warm or at room temperature as a delicious appetizer, snack, or part of a brunch spread.

NUTRITION

Cal 250; Fat 17 g; Carb 15 g;
Protein 10 g; Fiber: 3 g; Sodium: 440 mg

BEEF & LAMB RECIPES

Beef Kebabs

| Prep time: 15 min | Cook time 10 min | Serving: 2 |

INGREDIENTS

- *1 lb (450g) beef sirloin, cut into cubes*
- *1 bell pepper, cut into chunks*
- *1 onion, cut into chunks*
- *1 cup cherry tomatoes*
- *2 tablespoons olive oil*
- *2 cloves garlic, minced*
- *2 tablespoons lemon juice*
- *1 teaspoon dried oregano*
- *Salt and black pepper, to taste*
- *Greek yogurt tzatziki sauce, for serving*

1) In a bowl, whisk together olive oil, minced garlic, lemon juice, dried oregano, salt, and black pepper to make the marinade.
2) Place the beef cubes in a shallow dish or resealable plastic bag. Pour the marinade over the beef cubes, ensuring they are well coated. Cover or seal and refrigerate for at least 1 hour, or up to overnight, to allow the flavors to infuse.
3) If using wooden skewers, soak them in water for at least 30 minutes to prevent burning.
4) Preheat your grill to medium-high heat.
5) Thread the marinated beef cubes onto skewers, alternating with bell pepper chunks, onion chunks, and cherry tomatoes.
6) Grill the beef kebabs for about 3-4 minutes per side or until the beef is cooked to your desired doneness and the vegetables are tender and slightly charred.
7) Once the beef kebabs are cooked through, remove them from the grill and let them rest for a few minutes.

NUTRITION

Cal 350; Fat 20 g; Carb 9 g; Protein 35 g; Fiber: 2 g; Sodium: 150 mg

Greek Style Grilled Lamb Chops

Prep time: 10 min	Cook time 10 min	Serving: 2

INGREDIENTS

- *4 lamb chops*
- *2 tablespoons olive oil*
- *2 tablespoons lemon juice*
- *3 cloves garlic, minced*
- *1 teaspoon dried rosemary*
- *1 teaspoon dried oregano*
- *Salt and black pepper, to taste*
- *Greek yogurt tzatziki sauce, for serving*

1) In a bowl, whisk together olive oil, lemon juice, minced garlic, dried rosemary, dried oregano, salt, and black pepper to make the marinade.

2) Place the lamb chops in a shallow dish or resealable plastic bag. Pour the marinade over the lamb chops, ensuring they are well coated. Cover or seal and refrigerate for at least 1 hour, or up to overnight, to allow the flavors to infuse.

3) Preheat your grill to medium-high heat.

4) Remove the lamb chops from the marinade and discard any excess mar-inade.

5) Place the lamb chops on the preheated grill. Grill for about 3-4 minutes per side for medium-rare, or adjust the cooking time according to your desired doneness.

6) Once the lamb chops are cooked to your liking, remove them from the grill and let them rest for a few minutes.

7) Serve the Greek Style Grilled Lamb Chops hot, with Greek yogurt tzat-ziki sauce on the side.

NUTRITION

Cal 350; Fat 24 g; Carb 2 g; Protein 30 g; Fiber: 0 g; Sodium: 140 mg

Stewed Beef in Tomato Sauce

| Prep time: 10 min | Cook time 70 min | Serving: 2 |

INGREDIENTS

- *1/2 beef stew meat, cut into bite-sized pieces*
- *1 tablespoon olive oil*
- *1 small onion, diced*
- *1 clove garlic, minced*
- *1/2 cup beef broth*
- *1 can (14.5 ounces) diced tomatoes*
- *1 teaspoon tomato paste*
- *1/2 teaspoon dried thyme*
- *1/2 teaspoon dried oregano*
- *Salt and black pepper, to taste*
- *Chopped fresh parsley, for garnish (optional)*

1) Heat olive oil in a medium-sized pot over medium heat.
2) Add the diced onion and minced garlic to the pot, and sauté until the onion is softened and translucent, about 3-5 minutes.
3) Add the beef stew meat to the pot and brown on all sides, about 5-7 minutes.
4) Pour in the beef broth and diced tomatoes (with their juices) into the pot. Stir in the tomato paste, dried thyme, dried oregano, salt, and black pepper.
5) Bring the mixture to a simmer, then reduce the heat to low. Cover the pot and let it simmer gently for 1 to 1 1/2 hours or until the beef is tender and the sauce has thickened.
6) Check the seasoning and adjust salt and pepper if needed.
7) Serve the hearty stewed beef hot, garnished with chopped fresh parsley if desired.

NUTRITION

Cal 320; Fat 20 g; Carb 10 g;
Protein 25 g; Fiber: 2 g; Sodium: 400 mg

Lamb Meatballs

Prep time: 15 min | **Cook time:** 20 min | **Serving:** 2

INGREDIENTS

- *1 pound ground lamb*
- *1/4 cup breadcrumbs*
- *1/4 cup finely chopped onion*
- *2 cloves garlic, minced*
- *1 teaspoon ground cumin*
- *1 teaspoon ground coriander*
- *1/2 teaspoon smoked paprika*
- *1/4 teaspoon ground cinnamon*
- *Salt and pepper to taste*
- *1 egg, beaten*
- *2 tablespoons chopped fresh parsley*
- *2 tablespoons olive oil*
- *Lemon wedges, for serving*

1) Preheat the oven to 375°F (190°C).
2) In a large mixing bowl, combine the ground lamb, breadcrumbs, chopped onion, minced garlic, ground cumin, ground coriander, smoked paprika, ground cinnamon, salt, pepper, beaten egg, and chopped fresh parsley. Mix until well combined.
3) Shape the mixture into meatballs, about 1 to 1.5 inches in diameter.
4) Heat the olive oil in a large oven-safe skillet over medium-high heat.
5) Add the meatballs to the skillet and cook until browned on all sides, about 3-4 minutes.
6) Transfer the skillet to the preheated oven and bake for 10-12 minutes or until the meatballs are cooked through.
7) Once cooked, remove the skillet from the oven and let the meatballs rest for a few minutes before serving.
8) Serve the lamb meatballs hot with lemon wedges on the side for squeezing over the meatballs.

NUTRITION

Cal 280; Fat 18 g; Carb 5 g; Protein 24 g; Fiber: 1 g; Sodium: 420 mg

Tender Lamb Shanks

Prep time: 15 min	Cook time 2 hours 30 min	Serving: 4

INGREDIENTS

-) 4 lamb shanks
- Salt and black pepper to taste
- 2 tablespoons olive oil
- 1 onion, finely chopped
- 3 cloves garlic, minced
- 1 carrot, diced
- 1 celery stalk, diced
- 1 cup diced tomatoes
- 1 cup beef or vegetable broth
- 1/2 cup red wine (optional)
- 2 sprigs fresh rosemary
- 2 sprigs fresh thyme
- 1 bay leaf
- 1 tablespoon tomato paste
- Chopped fresh parsley, for garnish (optional)

1) Preheat the oven to 325°F (160°C).
2) Season the lamb shanks generously with salt and black pepper.
3) Heat the olive oil in a large oven-safe Dutch oven or braising pan over medium-high heat.
4) Brown the lamb shanks on all sides until deeply golden, about 3-4 minutes per side. Remove the shanks from the pan and set aside.
5) In the same pan, add the chopped onion, minced garlic, diced carrot, and diced celery. Cook, stirring occasionally, until the vegetables are softened, about 5 minutes.
6) Stir in the diced tomatoes, beef or vegetable broth, red wine (if using), fresh rosemary, fresh thyme, bay leaf, and tomato paste.
7) Return the lamb shanks to the pan, nestling them into the sauce.
8) Cover the pan with a lid and transfer it to the preheated oven.
9) Bake for 2 to 2 1/2 hours or until the lamb is tender and falling off the bone.
10) Remove the pan from the oven and discard the rosemary sprigs, thyme sprigs, and bay leaf.
11) Serve the tender lamb shanks hot, garnished with chopped fresh parsley if desired.
12) Optionally, serve the lamb shanks with couscous, rice, or crusty bread to soak up the flavorful sauce.

NUTRITION

Cal 450; Fat 25 g; Carb 10 g;
Protein 40 g; Fiber: 2 g; Sodium: 80 mg

Pulled Lamb Shoulder

Prep time: 15 min	Cook time 4 hours	Serving: 6

INGREDIENTS

- *1 bone-in lamb shoulder (about 4-5 pounds)*
- *Salt and black pepper, to taste*
- *2 tablespoons olive oil*
- *1 onion, sliced*
- *4 cloves garlic, minced*
- *1 tablespoon dried oregano*
- *1 tablespoon dried thyme*
- *1 teaspoon ground cumin*
- *1/2 teaspoon smoked paprika*
- *1/2 cup chicken or beef broth*
- *Juice of 1 lemon*
- *1/4 cup chopped fresh parsley, for garnish*

1) Preheat your oven to 325°F (160°C).
2) Season the lamb shoulder generously with salt and black pepper on all sides.
3) Heat the olive oil in a large Dutch oven or oven-safe pot over medium-high heat.
4) Sear the lamb shoulder on all sides until deeply browned, about 3-4 minutes per side. Remove the lamb shoulder from the pot and set aside.
5) In the same pot, add the sliced onion and minced garlic. Cook until the onion is softened and translucent, about 5 minutes.
6) Stir in the dried oregano, dried thyme, ground cumin, and smoked pap-rika. Cook for an additional 1-2 minutes until fragrant.
7) Return the lamb shoulder to the pot, nestling it into the onion and spice mixture.
8) Pour the chicken or beef broth and lemon juice over the lamb shoulder.
9) Cover the pot with a lid and transfer it to the preheated oven.
10) Roast the lamb shoulder for 3 1/2 to 4 hours or until the meat is tender and easily falls apart with a fork.
11) Once cooked, remove the lamb shoulder from the pot and let it rest for a few minutes.
12) Using two forks, shred the meat from the bone.
13) Serve the pulled lamb shoulder be hot, garnished with chopped fresh parsley.

NUTRITION

Cal 380; Fat 24 g; Carb 2 g; Protein 38 g; Fiber: 0 g; Sodium: 320 mg

Beef and Prunes

| Prep time: 2 min | Cook time 2 hours | Serving: 4 |

INGREDIENTS

- ***For the Beef and Prunes**:*
- *1.5 pounds beef chuck roast, cut into large cubes*
- *Salt and black pepper, to taste*
- *2 tablespoons olive oil*
- *1 onion, chopped*
- *3 cloves garlic, minced*
- *1 cup beef broth*
- *1 cup red wine (optional)*
- *1 cup pitted prunes*
- *2 tablespoons balsamic vinegar*
- *1 tablespoon honey*
- *2 bay leaves*
- *1 teaspoon dried thyme*
- *1 teaspoon dried rosemary*
- ***For the Sweet Carrots:***
- *4 large carrots, peeled and sliced into sticks*
- *2 tablespoons honey*
- *1 tablespoon olive oil*
- *Salt and black pepper, to taste*

1) Preheat your oven to 325°F (160°C).

2) Season the beef chuck roast cubes with salt and black pepper.

3) Heat the olive oil in a large oven-safe Dutch oven or pot over medium-high heat. Brown the beef cubes on all sides, working in batches if necessary. Remove the beef from the pot and set aside.

4) In the same pot, add the chopped onion and minced garlic. Cook until softened, about 5 minutes.

5) Return the beef to the pot. Add the beef broth, red wine (if using), pitted prunes, balsamic vinegar, honey, bay leaves, dried thyme, and dried rosemary. Stir to combine.

6) Cover the pot and transfer it to the preheated oven. Bake for 1 1/2 to 2 hours or until the beef is tender and the sauce has thickened.

7) While the beef is cooking, prepare the sweet carrots. In a bowl, toss the carrot sticks with honey, olive oil, salt, and black pepper. Spread them out on a baking sheet lined with parchment paper. Roast in the oven for 20-25 minutes or until caramelized and tender.

- *For the Crispy Rosemary Cracklin:*
- *2 sprigs fresh rosemary*
- *2 tablespoons olive oil*
- *Salt, to taste*

8) For the crispy rosemary cracklin, strip the leaves from the rosemary sprigs and chop them finely. In a small skillet, heat the olive oil over medium heat. Add the chopped rosemary leaves and fry until crispy, about 1-2 minutes. Remove from heat and drain on paper towels. Sprin-kle with salt.

9) Once the beef is done, remove the bay leaves and discard them.

10) Serve the beef and prunes hot, accompanied by the sweet carrots and sprinkled with crispy rosemary cracklin.

NUTRITION

Cal 450; Fat 20 g; Carb 35 g;
Protein 30 g; Fiber: 5 g; Sodium: 600 mg

Ground Beef Stir Fry

Prep time: 10 min | Cook time: 15 min | Serving: 2

INGREDIENTS

- *1/2 lb ground beef*
- *1 tablespoon olive oil*
- *2 cloves garlic, minced*
- *1/2 onion, thinly sliced*
- *1 bell pepper, thinly sliced*
- *1 small zucchini, thinly sliced*
- *1 teaspoon dried oregano*
- *1 teaspoon dried basil*
- *1/2 teaspoon paprika*
- *Salt and pepper, to taste*
- *2 tablespoons chopped fresh parsley, for garnish (optional)*
- *Lemon wedges, for serving*

1) Heat olive oil in a large skillet over medium-high heat.
2) Add minced garlic and sliced onion to the skillet. Cook until the onion is translucent, about 2-3 minutes.
3) Add ground beef to the skillet. Cook, breaking it up with a spatula, until it's browned and cooked through, about 5-7 minutes.
4) Stir in the sliced bell pepper and zucchini. Cook for an additional 3-4 minutes until the vegetables are tender-crisp.
5) Season the mixture with dried oregano, dried basil, paprika, salt, and pepper. Stir well to combine.
6) Cook for another minute to let the flavors meld together.
7) Remove the skillet from heat. Taste and adjust seasoning if needed.
8) Serve the Mediterranean Ground Beef Stir Fry hot, garnished with chopped fresh parsley if desired, and accompanied by lemon wedges for squeezing over the stir fry.

NUTRITION

Cal 380; Fat 25 g; Carb 10 g; Protein 30 g; Fiber: 2 g; Sodium: 520 mg

Mediterranean Steak Bites

Prep time: 10 min | Cook time: 10 min | Serving: 2

INGREDIENTS

- 1/2 lb ground beef
- 1 tablespoon olive oil
- 2 cloves garlic, minced
- 1/2 onion, thinly sliced
- 1 bell pepper, thinly sliced
- 1 small zucchini, thinly sliced
- 1 teaspoon dried oregano
- 1 teaspoon dried basil
- 1/2 teaspoon paprika
- Salt and pepper, to taste
- 2 tablespoons chopped fresh parsley for garnish (optional)
- Lemon wedges for serving

1) Season the bite-sized pieces of sirloin steak with salt and black pepper to taste.
2) In a large skillet, heat olive oil over medium-high heat.
3) Add minced garlic to the skillet and cook for about 30 seconds until fragrant.
4) Add the seasoned steak pieces to the skillet in a single layer. Let them cook without moving for about 2-3 minutes to get a nice sear on one side.
5) Flip the steak pieces to sear the other side for an additional 2-3 minutes or until they are cooked to your desired level of doneness.
6) Sprinkle dried oregano, dried thyme, paprika, and red pepper flakes (if using) over the steak bites. Toss to coat evenly.
7) Squeeze the juice of half a lemon over the steak bites and toss to combine.
8) Remove the skillet from heat and transfer the steak bites to a serving plate.
9) Garnish with chopped fresh parsley.
10) Serve the Mediterranean Steak Bites hot, with lemon wedges on the side for squeezing over the steak bites.

NUTRITION

Cal 320; Fat 20 g; Carb 2 g; Protein 30 g; Fiber: 2 g; Sodium: 440 mg

Steak Bowls

| Prep time: 15 min | Cook time 15 min | Serving: 2 |

INGREDIENTS

- **For the Steak:**
- *10 ounces (280g) sirloin steak*
- *Salt and black pepper, to taste*
- *1 tablespoon olive oil*
- *2 cloves garlic, minced*
- *1 teaspoon dried oregano*
- *1 teaspoon dried thyme*
- *1 teaspoon paprika*
- *1/4 teaspoon red pepper flakes (optional)*
- *Juice of 1/2 lemon*
- *2 tablespoons chopped fresh parsley for garnish*
- *Lemon wedges for serving*
- **For the Bowls:**
- *2 cups cooked quinoa or brown rice*
- *1 cup cherry tomatoes, halved*
- *1/2 English cucumber, diced*
- *1/4 cup Kalamata olives, sliced*
- *1/4 cup crumbled feta cheese*
- *2 tablespoons chopped fresh parsley for garnish*
- *Hummus for serving (optional)*

1) Season the sirloin steak with salt and black pepper to taste.
2) In a small bowl, combine minced garlic, dried oregano, dried thyme, paprika, and red pepper flakes (if using).
3) Rub the seasoning mixture onto both sides of the steak.
4) Heat olive oil in a skillet over medium-high heat.

NUTRITION
Cal 500; Fat 25 g; Carb 25 g;
Protein 35 g; Fiber: 6 g Sodium: 780 mg

Beef Cacciatore

| | Prep time: 15 min | | Cook time 2 hours | | Serving: 4 |

INGREDIENTS

- 1.5 pounds beef stew meat, cut into cubes
- Salt and black pepper, to taste
- 2 tablespoons olive oil
- 1 onion, chopped
- 2 cloves garlic, minced
- 1 bell pepper, sliced
- 1 cup sliced mushrooms
- 1 can (14.5 ounces) diced tomatoes
- 1/2 cup beef broth
- 1/4 cup red wine (optional)
- 1 teaspoon dried oregano
- 1 teaspoon dried basil
- 1/2 teaspoon dried thyme
- 1/4 teaspoon red pepper flakes (optional)
- 1/4 cup chopped fresh parsley for garnish
- Cooked pasta or crusty bread for serving

1) Season the beef stew meat with salt and black pepper.

2) Heat olive oil in a large skillet or Dutch oven over medium-high heat.

3) Add the seasoned beef cubes to the skillet and brown them on all sides, about 5-7 minutes. Work in batches if necessary to avoid overcrowding the pan. Remove the beef from the skillet and set aside.

4) In the same skillet, add chopped onion and minced garlic. Cook until softened and fragrant, about 3-4 minutes.

5) Add sliced bell pepper and mushrooms to the skillet. Cook for an addi-tional 3-4 minutes until the vegetables are tender.

6) Return the browned beef cubes to the skillet.

7) Pour in diced tomatoes (with their juices), beef broth, and red wine (if using). Stir to combine.

8) Add dried oregano, dried basil, dried thyme, and red pepper flakes (if using). Stir well to incorporate the spices.

9) Bring the mixture to a simmer, then reduce the heat to low. Cover and let it simmer gently for about 1 1/2 to 2 hours or until the beef is tender and the sauce has thickened.

10) Taste and adjust seasoning if necessary.
11) Serve the Mediterranean Beef Cacciatore hot, garnished with chopped fresh parsley. Serve over cooked pasta or with crusty bread for dipping.

NUTRITION
Cal 380; Fat 20 g; Carb 10 g;
Protein 35 g; Fiber: 2 g; Sodium: 620 mg

Moussaka

| Prep time: 30 min | Cook time 1 hours | Serving: 6 |

INGREDIENTS

- **For the Eggplant Layer:**
- 2 large eggplants, sliced lengthwise into 1/4-inch thick slices
- Salt
- Olive oil for brushing
- **For the Meat Sauce:**
- 1 tablespoon olive oil
- 1 onion, finely chopped
- 3 cloves garlic, minced
- 1 pound ground lamb or beef
- 1 can (14.5 ounces) diced tomatoes
- 2 tablespoons tomato paste
- 1 teaspoon dried oregano
- 1 teaspoon dried basil
- Salt and black pepper, to taste
- **For the Bechamel Sauce:**
- 4 tablespoons unsalted butter
- 1/4 cup all-purpose flour

1) Preheat your oven to 400°F (200°C). Place the eggplant slices on a bak-ing sheet lined with paper towels. Sprinkle salt over the slices and let them sit for about 15-20 minutes to draw out excess moisture.

2) After 15-20 minutes, pat the eggplant slices dry with paper towels to remove the excess moisture.

3) Brush both sides of the eggplant slices with olive oil. Place them on a baking sheet lined with parchment paper. Bake in the preheated oven for about 20-25 minutes or until the slices are golden and tender. Remove from the oven and set aside.

4) While the eggplant is baking, prepare the meat sauce. Heat olive oil in a large skillet over medium heat. Add chopped onion and minced garlic. Cook until softened and fragrant, about 3-4 minutes.

5) Add ground lamb or beef to the skillet. Cook until browned, breaking it up with a spoon as it cooks.

6) Stir in diced tomatoes, tomato paste, dried oregano, dried basil, salt, and black pepper. Simmer for about 15-20 minutes until the sauce thickens. Remove from heat and set aside.

7) To make the bechamel sauce, melt butter in a saucepan over medium heat. Whisk in all-purpose flour and cook for 1-2 minutes until the mix-ture turns golden brown.

- *2 cups milk*
- *Salt and black pepper, to taste*
- *Pinch of nutmeg*
- *1/2 cup grated Parmesan cheese*

8) Gradually whisk in milk, stirring constantly to prevent lumps from forming. Cook until the sauce thickens, about 5-7 minutes.

9) Season the bechamel sauce with salt, black pepper, and a pinch of nut-meg.

10) Remove the saucepan from heat and stir in grated Parmesan cheese until melted and smooth.

11) To assemble the moussaka, grease a 9x13-inch baking dish. Arrange half of the baked eggplant slices on the bottom of the dish.

12) Spread the meat sauce evenly over the eggplant layer.

13) Arrange the remaining eggplant slices over the meat sauce.

14) Pour the bechamel sauce over the top, spreading it out evenly.

15) Bake the moussaka in the preheated oven for about 30-35 minutes, or until the top is golden and bubbly.

16) Remove from the oven and let it cool for a few minutes before serving.

NUTRITION

Cal 450; Fat 30 g; Carb 20 g;
Protein 20 g; Fiber: 5 g; Sodium: 600 mg

Lamb Souvlaki

Prep time: 20 min	Cook time 70 min	Serving: 4

INGREDIENTS

- **For the Marinade:**
- 1/4 cup olive oil
- Juice of 1 lemon
- 3 cloves garlic, minced
- 1 teaspoon dried oregano
- 1 teaspoon dried thyme
- 1 teaspoon paprika
- Salt and black pepper, to taste
- **For the Lamb:**
- 1.5 pounds (680g) lamb leg or shoulder, cut into 1-inch cubes
- Wooden skewers, soaked in water for at least 30 minutes
- **For Serving:**
- Pita bread or flatbread
- Tzatziki sauce (see recipe above)
- Sliced tomatoes
- Sliced red onions
- Chopped fresh parsley
- Lemon wedges

1) In a large bowl, whisk together olive oil, lemon juice, minced garlic, dried oregano, dried thyme, paprika, salt, and black pepper to make the marinade.
2) Add the cubed lamb to the marinade and toss to coat evenly. Cover the bowl and refrigerate for at least 1 hour, or overnight for best results.
3) Preheat your grill or grill pan to medium-high heat.
4) Thread the marinated lamb cubes onto the soaked wooden skewers, leaving a little space between each piece.
5) Place the skewers on the preheated grill or grill pan. Cook for about 3-4 minutes on each side or until the lamb is cooked to your desired level of doneness and has a nice char on the outside.
6) Once cooked, remove the skewers from the grill and let them rest for a few minutes.
7) While the lamb is resting, warm the pita bread or flatbread on the grill for a minute on each side.
8) To serve, place a warmed pita bread or flatbread on a plate. Slide the cooked lamb off the skewers onto the bread.
9) Top the lamb with sliced tomatoes, sliced red onions, chopped fresh parsley, and a dollop of tzatziki sauce.
10) Serve the Lamb Souvlaki immediately, with lemon wedges on the side for squeezing over the souvlaki.

NUTRITION
Cal 350; Fat 20 g; Carb 5 g;
Protein 30 g; Fiber: 1 g; Sodium: 520 mg

Bifteki (Greek Beef Patties)

Prep time: 15 min | Cook time: 10 min | Serving: 2

INGREDIENTS

- *1/2 pound ground beef*
- *1/4 cup breadcrumbs*
- *1 small onion, finely chopped*
- *2 cloves garlic, minced*
- *1 egg*
- *1 tablespoon chopped fresh parsley*
- *1 teaspoon dried oregano*
- *Salt and black pepper, to taste*
- *2 tablespoons olive oil for cooking*
- **For Serving:**
- *Tzatziki sauce (see recipe above)*
- *Greek salad (tomatoes, cucumbers, red onions, olives, feta cheese)*
- *Pita bread or crusty bread*

1) In a mixing bowl, combine the ground beef, breadcrumbs, chopped on-ion, minced garlic, egg, chopped parsley, dried oregano, salt, and black pepper. Mix well until all ingredients are evenly incorporated.

2) Divide the mixture into two equal portions and shape each portion into a round patty, about 1/2 to 3/4 inch thick.

3) Heat olive oil in a skillet over medium-high heat.

4) Once the skillet is hot, add the beef patties. Cook for about 4-5 minutes on each side or until they are browned and cooked through to your desired level of doneness.

5) Remove the bifteki from the skillet and let them rest for a few minutes.

6) Serve the bifteki hot with tzatziki sauce, Greek salad, and pita bread or crusty bread on the side.

NUTRITION
Cal 400;Fat 30 g; Carb 5 g;
Protein 25 g; Fiber: 1 g; Sodium: 620 mg

Greek-Style Beef Stuffed Portobello Mushrooms

| Prep time: 20 min | Cook time 20 min | Serving: 4 |

INGREDIENTS

- *4 large portobello mushrooms*
- *1 pound lean ground beef*
- *1 tablespoon olive oil*
- *1 small onion, finely chopped*
- *2 cloves garlic, minced*
- *1/2 red bell pepper, finely chopped*
- *1/2 cup crumbled feta cheese*
- *1/4 cup chopped fresh parsley*
- *1 teaspoon dried oregano*
- *Salt and black pepper, to taste*
- *Lemon wedges for serving*
- *Chopped fresh parsley for garnish*

1) Preheat your oven to 375°F (190°C). Line a baking sheet with parchment paper.

2) Remove the stems from the portobello mushrooms and gently scrape out the gills using a spoon to create space for the stuffing. Place the mush-rooms on the prepared baking sheet, gill-side up.

3) In a skillet, heat olive oil over medium heat. Add chopped onion and minced garlic. Cook until softened and fragrant, about 3-4 minutes.

4) Add ground beef to the skillet. Cook until browned, breaking it up with a spoon as it cooks.

5) Stir in finely chopped red bell pepper, dried oregano, salt, and black pepper. Cook for an additional 2-3 minutes until the bell pepper is softened.

6) Remove the skillet from heat and let the mixture cool slightly.

7) Once cooled, stir in crumbled feta cheese and chopped fresh parsley.

8) Spoon the beef mixture into the portobello mushroom caps, dividing it evenly among the mushrooms.

9) Place the stuffed mushrooms in the preheated oven and bake for about 15-20 minutes or until the mushrooms are tender and the filling is cooked through.

10) Remove from the oven and let the stuffed mushrooms cool for a few minutes before serving.
11) Serve the Greek-style Beef Stuffed Portobello Mushrooms hot, garnished with chopped fresh parsley and accompanied by lemon wedges for squeezing over the mushrooms.

NUTRITION
Cal 320;Fat 18 g; Carb 10 g;
Protein 30 g; Fiber: 2 g; Sodium: 540 mg

POULTRY

Mediterranean Grilled Chicken

Prep time: 10 min | Cook time: 15 min | Serving: 2

INGREDIENTS

- *2 boneless, skinless chicken breasts*
- *2 tablespoons olive oil*
- *2 tablespoons lemon juice*
- *2 cloves garlic, minced*
- *1 teaspoon dried oregano*
- *1 teaspoon dried thyme*
- *Salt and black pepper, to taste*
- *Grilled vegetables for serving*

1) In a bowl, whisk together olive oil, lemon juice, minced garlic, dried oregano, dried thyme, salt, and black pepper to make the marinade.

2) Place the chicken breasts in a shallow dish or resealable plastic bag. Pour the marinade over the chicken, ensuring it is well coated. Cover or seal and refrigerate for at least 30 minutes, or up to 4 hours, to allow the flavors to infuse.

3) Preheat your grill to medium-high heat.

4) Remove the chicken breasts from the marinade and discard any excess marinade.

5) Place the chicken breasts on the preheated grill. Grill for about 6-8 minutes per side or until the chicken is cooked through and no longer pink in the center, with an internal temperature of 165°F (75°C).

6) While the chicken is grilling, you can also grill your favorite vegetables, such as bell peppers, zucchini, eggplant, or asparagus, for a delicious side dish.

7) Once the chicken is cooked through, remove it from the grill and let it rest for a few minutes before serving.

8) Serve the Mediterranean Grilled Chicken hot, with a side of grilled vegetables.

NUTRITION

Cal 220; Fat 10 g; Carb 1 g; Protein 28 g; Fiber: 0 g Sodium: 300 mg

Stuffed Chicken Breast

| Prep time: 15 min | Cook time 25 min | Serving: 2 |

INGREDIENTS

- 2 boneless, skinless chicken breasts
- 1 cup fresh spinach, chopped
- 1/4 cup sun-dried tomatoes, chopped
- 1/4 cup feta cheese, crumbled
- 2 tablespoons Kalamata olives, pitted, and sliced
- 1 tablespoon olive oil
- 1 teaspoon dried oregano
- Salt and black pepper, to taste
- Lemon wedges for serving
- Side salad for serving

1) Preheat your oven to 375°F (190°C).
2) Butterfly the chicken breasts by making a horizontal cut through the thickest part without cutting all the way through. Open the chicken breasts like a book.
3) In a bowl, combine chopped spinach, sun-dried tomatoes, feta cheese, Kalamata olives, olive oil, dried oregano, salt, and black pepper. Mix well.
4) Spoon the spinach mixture onto one side of each butterflied chicken breast.
5) Fold the other side of the chicken breast over the spinach mixture, creating a stuffed chicken breast.
6) Secure the edges with toothpicks if needed.
7) Place the stuffed chicken breasts in a baking dish.
8) Bake in the preheated oven for 20-25 minutes or until the chicken is cooked through and no longer pink in the center, with an internal temperature of 165°F (75°C).
9) While the chicken is baking, prepare a side salad for serving.
10) Once the chicken is cooked through, remove it from the oven and let it rest for a few minutes.
11) Serve the Mediterranean Stuffed Chicken Breast hot, with lemon wedges on the side for squeezing over and a refreshing side salad.

NUTRITION
Cal 280; Fat 15 g; Carb 5 g;
Protein 30 g; Fiber: 2 g Sodium: 450 mg

Balsamic Glazed Chicken Thighs

| | Prep time: 10 min | | Cook time 25 min | | Serving: 2 |

INGREDIENTS

- *4 bone-in, skin-on chicken thighs*
- *1/4 cup balsamic vinegar*
- *2 tablespoons olive oil*
- *2 cloves garlic, minced*
- *1 teaspoon honey (optional, use a small amount or omit for reduced sugar)*
- *Salt and black pepper, to taste*
- *Roasted vegetables for serving*

1) In a bowl, whisk together balsamic vinegar, olive oil, minced garlic, honey (if using), salt, and black pepper to make the marinade.

2) Place the chicken thighs in a shallow dish or resealable plastic bag. Pour the marinade over the chicken thighs, ensuring they are well coated. Cover or seal and refrigerate for at least 1 hour, or up to overnight, to allow the flavors to infuse.

3) Preheat your grill to medium-high heat or preheat your oven to 400°F (200°C).

4) If grilling, remove the chicken thighs from the marinade and discard any excess marinade. Grill the chicken thighs for about 10-12 minutes per side or until they are cooked through and caramelized, with an internal temperature of 165°F (75°C).

5) If baking, place the chicken thighs on a baking sheet lined with parchment paper or greased foil. Bake in the preheated oven for 20-25 minutes or until the chicken is cooked through and caramelized, with an internal temperature of 165°F (75°C).

6) While the chicken is cooking, you can prepare your favorite roasted vegetables as a side dish.

7) Once the chicken thighs are cooked through and caramelized, remove them from the grill or oven and let them rest for a few minutes.

8) Serve the Balsamic Glazed Chicken Thighs hot, with roasted vegetables on the side.

NUTRITION

Cal 380; Fat 25 g; Carb 4 g;
Protein 30 g; Fiber: 0 g Sodium: 210 mg

Turkey Meatballs

| Prep time: 15 min | Cook time: 20 min | Serving: 2 |

INGREDIENTS

- *1/2 lb (about 225g) ground turkey*
- *2 cloves garlic, minced*
- *1/4 cup onion, finely chopped*
- *2 tablespoons fresh parsley, chopped*
- *1 teaspoon dried oregano*
- *1/4 cup almond flour (or breadcrumbs for traditional version)*
- *Salt and black pepper, to taste*
- *Olive oil, for greasing*
- *Marinara sauce for serving*
- *Roasted vegetables for serving*

1) Preheat your oven to 400°F (200°C). Grease a baking sheet with olive oil or line it with parchment paper.
2) In a mixing bowl, combine the ground turkey, minced garlic, chopped onion, chopped parsley, dried oregano, almond flour (or breadcrumbs), salt, and black pepper. Mix until well combined.
3) Shape the mixture into meatballs, using about 1 tablespoon of the mix-ture for each meatball. Roll the mixture between your hands to form uniform-sized meatballs.
4) Place the meatballs on the prepared baking sheet, leaving some space between them.
5) Bake the meatballs in the preheated oven for 15-20 minutes or until they are cooked through and browned on the outside.
6) While the meatballs are baking, you can prepare your favorite roasted vegetables as a side dish.
7) Once the meatballs are cooked through, remove them from the oven and let them rest for a few minutes.
8) Serve the Mediterranean Turkey Meatballs hot, with marinara sauce drizzled over the top and roasted vegetables on the side.

NUTRITION
Cal 230; Fat 12 g; Carb 7 g;
Protein 22 g; Fiber: 2 g Sodium: 300 mg

Greek Style Lemon Chicken Skewers

Prep time: 15 min	Cook time 10 min	Serving: 2

INGREDIENTS

- *2 boneless, skinless chicken breasts, cut into cubes*
- *1/4 cup fresh lemon juice*
- *2 tablespoons olive oil*
- *2 cloves garlic, minced*
- *1 teaspoon dried oregano*
- *1/2 teaspoon paprika*
- *Salt and black pepper, to taste*
- *Wooden skewers, soaked in water for 30 minutes*
- *Greek salad for serving*

1) In a bowl, whisk together fresh lemon juice, olive oil, minced garlic, dried oregano, paprika, salt, and black pepper to make the marinade.
2) Place the chicken breast cubes in a shallow dish or resealable plastic bag. Pour the marinade over the chicken cubes, ensuring they are well coated. Cover or seal and refrigerate for at least 1 hour, or up to over-night, to allow the flavors to infuse.
3) Preheat your grill to medium-high heat.
4) Thread the marinated chicken cubes onto the soaked wooden skewers, dividing them evenly among the skewers.
5) Grill the chicken skewers for about 4-5 minutes per side or until the chicken is cooked through and has nice grill marks.
6) While the chicken skewers are grilling, prepare the Greek salad by combining diced cucumbers, tomatoes, red onions, bell peppers, Kala-mata olives, and feta cheese in a bowl. Dress with olive oil, lemon juice, dried oregano, salt, and black pepper, to taste.
7) Once the chicken skewers are cooked through, remove them from the grill and let them rest for a few minutes.
8) Serve the Greek Style Lemon Chicken Skewers hot, with a side of Greek salad
9) Serve the Greek Style Lemon Chicken Skewers hot, with a side of Greek salad

NUTRITION

Cal 250; Fat 12 g; Carb 4 g; Protein 30 g; Fiber: 1 g Sodium: 350 mg

Mediterranean Turkey Stuffed Bell Peppers

Prep time: 15 min | Cook time 40 min | Serving: 2

INGREDIENTS

- *2 large bell peppers, halved and seeds removed*
- *1/2 lb ground turkey*
- *1 cup diced tomatoes (canned or fresh)*
- *1 cup fresh spinach, chopped*
- *1/4 cup sliced black olives*
- *1/4 cup crumbled feta cheese*
- *2 cloves garlic, minced*
- *1 teaspoon dried oregano*
- *1/2 teaspoon dried basil*
- *Salt and black pepper, to taste*
- *Olive oil for drizzling*

1) Preheat your oven to 375°F (190°C).
2) In a skillet over medium heat, cook the ground turkey until it's browned and cooked through. Drain any excess fat if necessary.
3) Add minced garlic to the skillet and cook for 1-2 minutes until fragrant.
4) Stir in diced tomatoes, chopped spinach, sliced black olives, dried oregano, dried basil, salt, and black pepper. Cook for another 2-3 minutes, allowing the flavors to meld together.
5) Remove the skillet from heat and stir in crumbled feta cheese.
6) Arrange the halved bell peppers in a baking dish, cut side up.
7) Spoon the turkey mixture into each bell pepper half, pressing down gently to pack the filling.
8) Drizzle olive oil over the stuffed bell peppers and cover the baking dish with aluminum foil.
9) Bake in the preheated oven for 30-35 minutes or until the bell peppers are tender and the filling is heated through.
10) Remove the foil and bake for an additional 5 minutes to lightly brown the tops of the peppers.
11) Once cooked, remove from the oven and let them cool slightly before serving.
12) Serve the Mediterranean Turkey Stuffed Bell Peppers hot as a flavorful and nutritious main course.

NUTRITION

Cal 260; Fat 12 g; Carb 15 g;
Protein 22 g; Fiber: 5 g Sodium: 460 mg

Spanish-Style Chicken Casserole

Prep time: 20 min | Cook time: 60 min | Serving: 4

INGREDIENTS

- *4 boneless, skinless chicken breasts*
- *Salt and black pepper, to taste*
- *2 tablespoons olive oil*
- *1 onion, chopped*
- *3 cloves garlic, minced*
- *1 bell pepper, sliced*
- *1 zucchini, sliced*
- *1 cup sliced mushrooms*
- *1 can (14.5 ounces) diced tomatoes*
- *1/2 cup chicken broth*
- *1 teaspoon smoked paprika*
- *1 teaspoon dried oregano*
- *1/2 teaspoon dried thyme*
- *1/4 teaspoon red pepper flakes (optional)*
- *1/4 cup chopped fresh parsley for garnish*

1) Preheat your oven to 375°F (190°C).
2) Season the chicken breasts with salt and black pepper to taste.
3) Heat olive oil in a large oven-safe skillet or Dutch oven over medium-high heat.
4) Add the seasoned chicken breasts to the skillet and brown them on both sides, about 3-4 minutes per side. Remove the chicken from the skillet and set aside.
5) In the same skillet, add chopped onion and minced garlic. Cook until softened and fragrant, about 3-4 minutes.
6) Add sliced bell pepper, sliced zucchini, and sliced mushrooms to the skillet. Cook for an additional 4-5 minutes until the vegetables are slightly softened.
7) Stir in diced tomatoes (with their juices), chicken broth, smoked papri-ka, dried oregano, dried thyme, and red pepper flakes (if using). Bring the mixture to a simmer.
8) Return the browned chicken breasts to the skillet, nestling them into the vegetable mixture.
9) Cover the skillet or Dutch oven with a lid or aluminum foil and transfer it to the preheated oven.
10) Bake for about 30-40 minutes or until the chicken is cooked through and tender.
11) Once cooked, remove the skillet from the oven and let it cool for a few minutes.

12) Garnish the Spanish-Style Chicken Casserole with chopped fresh parsley before serving.

13) Serve hot, either on its own or with crusty bread or cooked rice to soak up the delicious sauce.

NUTRITION
Cal 380; Fat 15 g; Carb 25 g;
Protein 30 g; Fiber: 5 g Sodium: 620 mg

Chicken Skillet

Prep time: 10 min	Cook time 20 min	Serving: 2

INGREDIENTS

- *2 boneless, skinless chicken breasts, cut into bite-sized pieces*
- *Salt and black pepper, to taste*
- *2 tablespoons olive oil*
- *2 cloves garlic, minced*
- *1/2 onion, diced*
- *1/2 red bell pepper, diced*
- *1/2 yellow bell pepper, diced*
- *1/2 cup cherry tomatoes, halved*
- *1/4 cup Kalamata olives, pitted and halved*
- *1 teaspoon dried oregano*
- *1/2 teaspoon dried thyme*
- *1/4 teaspoon red pepper flakes (optional)*
- *Juice of 1/2 lemon*
- *2 tablespoons chopped fresh parsley for garnish*

1) Season the chicken breast pieces with salt and black pepper to taste.
2) Heat olive oil in a large skillet over medium-high heat.
3) Add minced garlic to the skillet and cook for about 30 seconds until fragrant.
4) Add diced onion, diced red bell pepper, and diced yellow bell pepper to the skillet. Cook until softened, about 3-4 minutes.
5) Add the seasoned chicken breast pieces to the skillet. Cook until browned on all sides and cooked through, about 5-7 minutes.
6) Stir in halved cherry tomatoes, halved Kalamata olives, dried oregano, dried thyme, and red pepper flakes (if using). Cook for an additional 2-3 minutes until the tomatoes are slightly softened.
7) Squeeze the juice of half a lemon over the skillet and stir to combine.
8) Remove the skillet from heat and garnish with chopped fresh parsley.
9) Serve the Mediterranean Chicken Skillet hot, either on its own or with a side of cooked quinoa, couscous, or crusty bread.

NUTRITION

Cal 380; Fat 20 g; Carb 15 g;
Protein 30 g; Fiber: 3 g Sodium: 620 mg

Chicken Piccata

Prep time: 10 min | **Cook time:** 15 min | **Serving:** 2

INGREDIENTS

- *2 boneless, skinless chicken breasts*
- *Salt and black pepper, to taste*
- *2 tablespoons all-purpose flour*
- *2 tablespoons olive oil*
- *2 cloves garlic, minced*
- *1/4 cup chicken broth*
- *2 tablespoons freshly squeezed lemon juice*
- *2 tablespoons capers, drained*
- *2 tablespoons chopped fresh parsley for garnish*
- *Lemon slices, for serving*

1) Place the chicken breasts between two pieces of plastic wrap. Use a meat mallet or the bottom of a heavy pan to pound them to an even thickness, about 1/2 inch thick. Season both sides of the chicken breasts with salt and black pepper.

2) Place the flour on a plate. Dredge the chicken breasts in the flour, shaking off any excess.

3) In a large skillet, heat the olive oil over medium-high heat. Add the chicken breasts to the skillet and cook until golden brown and cooked through, about 4-5 minutes per side. Remove the chicken from the skillet and set aside on a plate.

4) In the same skillet, add the minced garlic and cook for about 30 seconds until fragrant.

5) Pour in the chicken broth and lemon juice, stirring to scrape up any browned bits from the bottom of the skillet. Bring the mixture to a simmer.

6) Stir in the capers and let the sauce simmer for about 2-3 minutes, until slightly thickened.

7) Return the chicken breasts to the skillet, turning them in the sauce to coat evenly. Cook for an additional minute to heat through.

8) Garnish the Mediterranean Style Chicken Piccata with chopped fresh parsley.

9) Serve the chicken piccata hot, with lemon slices on the side for squeezing over the chicken.

NUTRITION

Cal 320; Fat 15 g; Carb 10 g; Protein 30 g; Fiber: 1 g Sodium: 520 mg

Mediterranean Turkey Bowls

| Prep time: 15 min | Cook time 20 min | Serving: 2 |

INGREDIENTS

- *For the Turkey Patties:*
- *8 ounces ground turkey*
- *1/4 cup breadcrumbs*
- *1 clove garlic, minced*
- *1 tablespoon chopped fresh parsley*
- *1 teaspoon dried oregano*
- *Salt and black pepper, to taste*
- *1 tablespoon olive oil*
- *For the Bowl:*
- *1 cup cooked quinoa*
- *1 cup cherry tomatoes, halved*
- *1/2 cucumber, diced*
- *1/4 cup Kalamata olives, pitted and halved*
- *2 tablespoons crumbled feta cheese*
- *2 tablespoons tzatziki sauce*
- *Lemon wedges for serving*

1) In a mixing bowl, combine ground turkey, breadcrumbs, minced garlic, chopped parsley, dried oregano, salt, and black pepper. Mix well until all ingredients are evenly incorporated.
2) Divide the turkey mixture into two equal portions. Shape each portion into a round patty.
3) Heat olive oil in a skillet over medium-high heat. Add the turkey patties to the skillet and cook for about 4-5 minutes on each side or until golden brown and cooked through.
4) While the turkey patties are cooking, prepare the remaining ingredients for the bowl.
5) Divide cooked quinoa between two serving bowls.
6) Top the quinoa with halved cherry tomatoes, diced cucumber, halved Kalamata olives, and crumbled feta cheese.
7) Once the turkey patties are cooked, place one patty on each bowl over the quinoa and vegetable mixture.
8) Drizzle tzatziki sauce over the turkey patties.
9) Serve the Mediterranean Turkey Bowls hot, with lemon wedges on the side for squeezing over the bowls.

NUTRITION
Cal 400; Fat 20 g; Carb 30 g;
Protein 25 g; Fiber: 7 g Sodium: 620 mg

Zucchini Stuffed with Turkey

Prep time: 20 min | Cook time: 40 min | Serving: 2

INGREDIENTS

- 2 medium zucchini
- 8 ounces ground turkey
- 1/2 onion, finely chopped
- 2 cloves garlic, minced
- 1/2 red bell pepper, diced
- 1/2 cup cherry tomatoes, halved
- 1/4 cup crumbled feta cheese
- 1/4 cup chopped fresh parsley
- 1 teaspoon dried oregano
- Salt and black pepper, to taste
- 2 tablespoons olive oil

1) Preheat your oven to 375°F (190°C). Grease a baking dish with olive oil or cooking spray.
2) Cut the zucchini in half lengthwise. Use a spoon to carefully scoop out the flesh from the center of each zucchini half, creating a hollow cavity. Reserve the flesh for later use.
3) Heat 1 tablespoon of olive oil in a skillet over medium heat. Add the chopped onion and minced garlic. Cook until softened and fragrant, about 3-4 minutes.
4) Add the ground turkey to the skillet. Cook until browned, breaking it up with a spoon as it cooks.
5) Stir in the diced red bell pepper and the reserved zucchini flesh. Cook for an additional 3-4 minutes.
6) Add the halved cherry tomatoes, crumbled feta cheese, chopped fresh parsley, dried oregano, salt, and black pepper to the skillet. Stir well to combine and cook for another 2-3 minutes.
7) Fill each hollowed-out zucchini half with the turkey mixture, pressing down gently to pack it in.
8) Place the stuffed zucchini halves in the greased baking dish. Drizzle with the remaining tablespoon of olive oil.
9) Cover the baking dish with aluminum foil and bake in the preheated oven for 30 minutes.

10) After 30 minutes, remove the foil and bake for an additional 10 minutes or until the zucchini is tender and the tops are lightly browned.
11) Serve the Mediterranean Zucchini Stuffed with Turkey hot, garnished with additional chopped parsley if desired.

NUTRITION

Cal 350; Fat 15 g; Carb 20 g;
Protein 30 g; Fiber: 5 g Sodium: 620 mg

Turkey Meatball and Orzo Bowl

| Prep time: 15 min | Cook time 30 min | Serving: 2 |

INGREDIENTS

- *For the Turkey Meatballs:*
- *8 ounces (225g) ground turkey*
- *1/4 cup breadcrumbs*
- *1/4 cup grated Parmesan cheese*
- *1/4 cup chopped fresh parsley*
- *1 clove garlic, minced*
- *1 teaspoon dried oregano*
- *Salt and black pepper, to taste*
- *1 tablespoon olive oil for cooking*
- *For the Orzo:*
- *1/2 cup dry orzo pasta*
- *1 cup chicken broth*
- *1/2 tablespoon olive oil*
- *1/4 teaspoon dried basil*
- *Salt and black pepper, to taste*
- *For Serving:*
- *1 cup cherry tomatoes, halved*
- *1/2 cucumber, diced*

1) Preheat your oven to 375°F (190°C). Line a baking sheet with parchment paper.

2) In a mixing bowl, combine ground turkey, breadcrumbs, grated Par-mesan cheese, chopped parsley, minced garlic, dried oregano, salt, and black pepper. Mix well until all ingredients are evenly incorporated.

3) Shape the turkey mixture into small meatballs, about 1 inch in diameter, and place them on the prepared baking sheet.

4) Drizzle the meatballs with olive oil. Bake in the preheated oven for about 20 minutes or until cooked through and golden brown.

5) While the meatballs are baking, cook the orzo according to package in-structions, using chicken broth instead of water for added flavor. Once cooked, drain any excess liquid.

6) In a skillet, heat 1/2 tablespoon of olive oil over medium heat. Add the cooked orzo to the skillet. Stir in dried basil, salt, and black pepper. Cook for a few minutes until heated through.

7) Divide the cooked orzo between two serving bowls.

8) Top the orzo with baked turkey meat-balls, halved cherry tomatoes, diced cucumber, halved Kalamata olives, and crumbled feta cheese.

- *1/4 cup Kalamata olives, pitted and halved*
- *2 tablespoons crumbled feta cheese*
- *Lemon wedges for serving*
- *Chopped fresh parsley for garnish*

9) Garnish the bowls with chopped fresh parsley and serve with lemon wedges on the side for squeezing over the bowls.

NUTRITION
Cal 400; Fat 15 g;Carb 40 g;
Protein 30 g; Fiber: 5 g Sodium: 620 mg

Couscous & Chicken Bake

| Prep time: 15 min | Cook time 35 min | Serving: 4 |

INGREDIENTS

- *1 cup couscous*
- *1 1/4 cups chicken broth*
- *1 tablespoon olive oil*
- *1 onion, chopped*
- *2 cloves garlic, minced*
- *1 red bell pepper, diced*
- *1 yellow bell pepper, diced*
- *1 zucchini, diced*
- *1 pound boneless, skinless chicken breasts, diced*
- *1 teaspoon dried oregano*
- *1 teaspoon dried thyme*
- *Salt and black pepper, to taste*
- *1 can (14.5 ounces) diced tomatoes, drained*
- *1/4 cup Kalamata olives, pitted and halved*
- *1/4 cup crumbled feta cheese*
- *Chopped fresh parsley for garnish*

1) Preheat your oven to 375°F (190°C). Grease a baking dish with olive oil or cooking spray.
2) In a saucepan, bring the chicken broth to a boil. Stir in the couscous, cover, and remove from heat. Let it sit for about 5 minutes, then fluff with a fork.
3) In a large skillet, heat olive oil over medium heat. Add chopped onion and minced garlic. Cook until softened and fragrant, about 3-4 minutes.
4) Add diced red bell pepper, diced yellow bell pepper, and diced zucchini to the skillet. Cook for an additional 4-5 minutes until the vegetables are slightly softened.
5) Add diced chicken breast to the skillet. Cook until browned on all sides and cooked through, about 5-7 minutes.
6) Stir in dried oregano, dried thyme, salt, and black pepper. Cook for another minute.
7) Remove the skillet from heat. Stir in the cooked couscous, drained diced tomatoes, and Kalamata olives until well combined.
8) Transfer the couscous and chicken mixture to the greased baking dish. Spread it out evenly.
9) Sprinkle crumbled feta cheese over the top of the mixture.
10) Bake in the preheated oven for about 20-25 minutes or until heated through and the cheese is melted and slightly golden.
11) Garnish with chopped fresh parsley before serving.

NUTRITION

Cal 380; Fat 12 g; Carb 35 g;
Protein 30 g; Fiber: 5 g Sodium: 580 mg

Baked Chicken Thighs in Yogurt Sauce with Herbs

Prep time: 10 min	Cook time 35 min	Serving: 2

INGREDIENTS

- *2 bone-in, skin-on chicken thighs*
- *Salt and black pepper, to taste*
- *1/2 cup Greek yogurt*
- *1 tablespoon olive oil*
- *2 cloves garlic, minced*
- *1 tablespoon chopped fresh parsley*
- *1 tablespoon chopped fresh dill*
- *1 tablespoon chopped fresh mint*
- *Zest of 1 lemon*
- *Juice of 1/2 lemon*
- *Lemon wedges for serving*

1) Preheat your oven to 375°F (190°C). Grease a baking dish with olive oil or cooking spray.

2) Season the chicken thighs generously with salt and black pepper.

3) In a mixing bowl, combine Greek yogurt, olive oil, minced garlic, chopped parsley, chopped dill, chopped mint, lemon zest, and lemon juice. Mix well until all ingredients are combined.

4) Place the chicken thighs in the greased baking dish. Spoon the yogurt mixture evenly over the chicken thighs, making sure to coat them completely.

5) Bake in the preheated oven for about 30-35 minutes or until the chicken thighs are cooked through and the skin is golden brown and crispy.

6) Once cooked, remove the chicken thighs from the oven and let them rest for a few minutes.

7) Serve the Baked Chicken Thighs in Yogurt Sauce with Herbs hot, garnished with additional chopped herbs if desired, and lemon wedges on the side for squeezing over the chicken.

NUTRITION

Cal 350; Fat 20 g; Carb 5 g; Protein 30 g; Fiber: 1 g Sodium: 550 mg

Mediterranean Turkey Meatloaf

| Prep time: 10 min | Cook time 40 min | Serving: 2 |

INGREDIENTS

- *8 ounces ground turkey*
- *1/4 cup breadcrumbs*
- *1/4 cup chopped fresh parsley*
- *1/4 cup chopped sun-dried tomatoes (packed in oil), drained*
- *1/4 cup crumbled feta cheese*
- *1 egg*
- *1 clove garlic, minced*
- *1/2 teaspoon dried oregano*
- *Salt and black pepper, to taste*
- *Olive oil for greasing*
- ***For the Glaze:***
- *2 tablespoons tomato paste*
- *1 tablespoon balsamic vinegar*
- *1 teaspoon honey*
- *1/2 teaspoon dried thyme*

1) Preheat your oven to 375°F (190°C). Grease a small loaf pan with olive oil.
2) In a mixing bowl, combine ground turkey, breadcrumbs, chopped parsley, chopped sun-dried tomatoes, crumbled feta cheese, egg, minced garlic, dried oregano, salt, and black pepper. Mix well until all in-gredients are evenly incorporated.
3) Press the turkey mixture into the prepared loaf pan, shaping it into a loaf shape.
4) In a small bowl, whisk together tomato paste, balsamic vinegar, honey, and dried thyme to make the glaze.
5) Spread the glaze evenly over the top of the meatloaf.
6) Bake in the preheated oven for about 35-40 minutes or until the meat-loaf is cooked through and the top is browned.
7) Once cooked, remove the meatloaf from the oven and let it rest for a few minutes before slicing.
8) Serve the Mediterranean Turkey Meat-loaf hot, sliced into thick slices.

NUTRITION
Cal 320; Fat 12 g; Carb 15 g; Protein 30 g; Fiber: 2 g Sodium: 620 mg

Turkey Wraps

| Prep time: 10 min | Cook time: 0 min | Serving: 2 |

INGREDIENTS

- *4 large whole wheat or whole grain wraps*
- *8 ounces chopped cooked turkey breast*
- *1/2 cup hummus*
- *1/2 cup chopped cucumber*
- *1/2 cup chopped tomato*
- *1/4 cup sliced red onion*
- *1/4 cup crumbled feta cheese*
- *1/4 cup chopped Kalamata olives*
- *2 tablespoons chopped fresh parsley*
- *Salt and black pepper, to taste*
- *Lemon wedges, for serving (optional)*

1) Lay out the wraps on a clean work surface.
2) Spread an even layer of hummus over each wrap, leaving a small border around the edges.
3) Divide the sliced turkey breast evenly among the wraps, placing it on top of the hummus.
4) Top the turkey with chopped cucumber, chopped tomato, sliced red onion, crumbled feta cheese, chopped Kalamata olives, and chopped fresh parsley.
5) Season with salt and black pepper to taste.
6) Roll up the wraps tightly, folding in the sides as you go to secure the fillings.
7) Slice each wrap in half diagonally to serve.
8) Serve the Mediterranean Turkey Wraps with lemon wedges on the side for squeezing over the wraps, if desired.

NUTRITION

Cal 380; Fat 15 g; Carb 35 g;
Protein 25 g; Fiber: 5 g; Sodium: 520 mg

Turkey Panini

| Prep time: 10 min | Cook time 5 min | Serving: 2 |

INGREDIENTS

- *4 slices whole grain bread*
- *8 ounces chopped cooked turkey breast*
- *1/2 cup baby spinach leaves*
- *1/4 cup roasted red peppers, sliced*
- *1/4 cup sliced Kalamata olives*
- *1/4 cup crumbled feta cheese*
- *2 tablespoons hummus*
- *1 tablespoon olive oil for brushing*

1) Preheat your panini press or grill pan.
2) Lay out the slices of bread on a clean work surface.
3) Spread hummus evenly on each slice of bread.
4) Divide the sliced turkey breast, baby spinach leaves, roasted red peppers, sliced Kalamata olives, and crumbled feta cheese evenly between two slices of bread.
5) Top each sandwich with the remaining slices of bread to form sand-wiches.
6) Brush the outsides of the sandwiches lightly with olive oil.
7) Place the sandwiches on the preheated panini press or grill pan. If using a grill pan, place a heavy skillet on top of the sandwiches to press them down.
8) Cook for about 3-4 minutes or until the bread is toasted and the fillings are heated through, and the turkey breast is cooked through.
9) Carefully remove the sandwiches from the panini press or grill pan.
10) Slice the sandwiches in half diagonally and serve hot.

NUTRITION

Cal 420; Fat 18 g; Carb 35 g;
Protein 30 g; Fiber: 5 g; Sodium: 780 mg

Turkey Pieces Baked in Pumpkin

| Prep time: 15 min | Cook time 60 min | Serving: 2 |

INGREDIENTS

- *1 small pumpkin (about 2 pounds), washed and top removed*
- *8 ounces turkey breast or thigh, cut into chunks*
- *1 onion, diced*
- *2 cloves garlic, minced*
- *1 bell pepper, diced*
- *1 tomato, diced*
- *1/4 cup chopped fresh parsley*
- *1 teaspoon dried oregano*
- *Salt and black pepper, to taste*
- *2 tablespoons olive oil*

1) Preheat your oven to 375°F (190°C).
2) Cut the top off the pumpkin and remove the seeds and stringy flesh from the center to create a hollow cavity.
3) In a bowl, combine the turkey pieces, diced onion, minced garlic, diced bell pepper, diced tomato, chopped fresh parsley, dried oregano, salt, black pepper, and olive oil. Mix well to coat the turkey and vegetables evenly with the seasoning.
4) Stuff the seasoned turkey and vegetable mixture into the hollowed-out pumpkin.
5) Place the stuffed pumpkin on a baking sheet lined with parchment paper.
6) Cover the pumpkin with its lid or loosely with aluminum foil.
7) Bake in the preheated oven for about 50-60 minutes or until the pump-kin is tender and the turkey is cooked through.
8) Remove the lid or foil during the last 10 minutes of baking to allow the top of the turkey to brown slightly.
9) Once cooked, carefully remove the pump-kin from the oven and let it cool for a few minutes before slicing and serving.
10) Serve the Turkey Pieces Baked in Pumpkin hot, scooping out portions of the tender pumpkin along with the turkey and vegetable filling.

NUTRITION

Cal 320; Fat 15 g; Carb 20 g;
Protein 30 g; Fiber: 5 g; Sodium: 620 mg

Duck Breast with Figs and Olives

Prep time: 10 min | Cook time 20 min | Serving: 2

INGREDIENTS

- *2 duck breasts, skin-on*
- *Salt and black pepper, to taste*
- *1 tablespoon olive oil*
- *6 fresh figs, halved*
- *1/4 cup Kalamata olives, pitted and halved*
- *2 cloves garlic, minced*
- *1/4 cup balsamic vinegar*
- *2 tablespoons honey*
- *1 teaspoon dried thyme*
- *1 teaspoon dried rosemary*
- *Chopped fresh parsley for garnish*

1) Preheat your oven to 400°F (200°C).
2) Score the skin of the duck breasts in a crosshatch pattern, being careful not to cut into the meat. Season both sides of the duck breasts with salt and black pepper.
3) Heat olive oil in an oven-safe skillet over medium-high heat. Once hot, add the duck breasts, skin side down. Cook for about 5 minutes until the skin is crispy and golden brown.
4) Flip the duck breasts and cook for an additional 2 minutes on the other side.
5) Remove the duck breasts from the skillet and set them aside on a plate.
6) In the same skillet, add halved figs, halved Kalamata olives, and minced garlic. Cook for 2-3 minutes, stirring occasionally until the figs start to soften.
7) Stir in balsamic vinegar, honey, dried thyme, and dried rosemary. Allow the mixture to come to a simmer.
8) Return the duck breasts to the skillet, skin side up, nestled among the figs and olives.
9) Transfer the skillet to the preheated oven and bake for about 10-12 minutes or until the duck breasts are cooked to your desired level of doneness.
10) Once cooked, remove the skillet from the oven. Let the duck breasts rest for a few minutes before slicing.
11) Serve the Mediterranean Duck Breast with Figs and Olives hot, garnished with chopped fresh parsley.

NUTRITION
Cal 450; Fat 25 g; Carb 20 g;
Protein 35 g; Fiber: 5 g; Sodium: 680 mg

Xinomavro Duck with Cornmeal Cream

Prep time: 15 min

Cook time: 60 min

Serving: 2

INGREDIENTS

- *2 duck breasts*
- *Salt and black pepper, to taste*
- *1 tablespoon olive oil*
- *1 onion, finely chopped*
- *2 cloves garlic, minced*
- *1/2 cup Xinomavro wine (or substitute red wine)*
- *1 cup chicken or vegetable broth*
- *1/4 cup heavy cream*
- *1/4 cup cornmeal*
- *2 tablespoons butter*
- *Chopped fresh parsley for garnish*

1) Preheat your oven to 375°F (190°C).

2) Score the skin of the duck breasts in a crosshatch pattern, being careful not to cut into the meat. Season both sides of the duck breasts with salt and black pepper.

3) Heat olive oil in an oven-safe skillet over medium-high heat. Once hot, add the duck breasts, skin side down. Cook for about 5 minutes until the skin is crispy and golden brown.

4) Flip the duck breasts and cook for an additional 2 minutes on the other side. Remove the duck breasts from the skillet and set them aside on a plate.

5) In the same skillet, add chopped onion and minced garlic. Cook for about 3-4 minutes until softened and fragrant.

6) Pour Xinomavro wine into the skillet, scraping up any browned bits from the bottom of the pan. Allow the wine to simmer for a few minutes to reduce slightly.

7) Stir in chicken or vegetable broth and bring the mixture to a simmer.

8) Return the duck breasts to the skillet, skin side up, nestled among the onions and garlic. Transfer the skillet to the preheated oven and roast for about 25-30 minutes or until the duck breasts are cooked to your desired level of doneness.

9) While the duck is roasting, prepare the cornmeal cream. In a small saucepan, heat heavy cream over medium heat until warm.
10) Gradually whisk in cornmeal, stirring constantly to prevent lumps from forming. Cook for about 5-7 minutes until the mixture thickens to a creamy consistency.
11) Stir in butter until melted and well incorporated into the cornmeal cream.
12) Once the duck is cooked, remove the skillet from the oven. Let the duck breasts rest for a few minutes before slicing.
13) Serve the Xinomavro Duck with Cornmeal Cream hot, drizzling the cornmeal cream over the sliced duck breasts. Garnish with chopped fresh parsley.

NUTRITION
Cal 480; Fat 28 g; Carb 25 g;
Protein 32 g; Fiber: 3 g; Sodium: 630 mg

Duck Breast with Honey and Spices

Prep time: 10 min | Cook time 20 min | Serving: 2

INGREDIENTS

- *2 duck breasts, skin-on*
- *Salt and black pepper, to taste*
- *2 tablespoons honey*
- *1 teaspoon ground cumin*
- *1 teaspoon ground coriander*
- *1/2 teaspoon smoked paprika*
- *1/4 teaspoon ground cinnamon*
- *1 tablespoon olive oil*
- *2 cloves garlic, minced*
- *1 tablespoon balsamic vinegar*
- *Chopped fresh parsley for garnish*

1) Preheat your oven to 375°F (190°C).

2) Score the skin of the duck breasts in a cross-hatch pattern, being careful not to cut into the meat. Season both sides of the duck breasts with salt and black pepper.

3) In a small bowl, combine honey, ground cumin, ground coriander, smoked paprika, and ground cinnamon to make a spice rub.

4) Rub the spice mixture all over the duck breasts, coating them evenly.

5) Heat olive oil in an oven-safe skillet over medium-high heat. Once hot, add the duck breasts, skin side down. Cook for about 5 minutes until the skin is crispy and golden brown.

6) Flip the duck breasts and add minced garlic to the skillet. Cook for an ad-ditional 2 minutes, until the garlic is fragrant.

7) Transfer the skillet to the preheated oven and roast for about 10-12 minutes or until the duck breasts are cooked to your desired level of doneness.

8) Remove the skillet from the oven and transfer the duck breasts to a cutting board. Let them rest for a few minutes before slicing.

9) While the duck is resting, place the skillet back on the stove over medium heat. Add balsamic vinegar to the skillet, scraping up any browned bits from the bottom of the pan. Cook for a minute or two until the sauce thickens slightly.

10) Slice the duck breasts and drizzle with the balsamic glaze.
11) Garnish with chopped fresh parsley and serve hot.

NUTRITION
Cal 420; Fat 28 g; Carb 10 g;
Protein 32 g; Fiber: 1 g; Sodium: 620 mg

SEAFOOD & FISH

Grilled Mediterranean Salmon

| Prep time: 10 min | Cook time: 10 min | Serving: 2 |

INGREDIENTS

- *2 salmon fillets (about 6 oz each)*
- *2 tablespoons olive oil*
- *Juice of 1 lemon*
- *2 cloves garlic, minced*
- *1 teaspoon dried oregano*
- *1 teaspoon dried thyme*
- *Salt and black pepper, to taste*
- *Lemon wedges for serving*
- *Fresh parsley for garnish (optional)*

1) In a shallow dish or resealable plastic bag, combine olive oil, lemon juice, minced garlic, dried oregano, dried thyme, salt, and black pepper to make the marinade.

2) Place the salmon fillets in the marinade, turning to coat them evenly. Cover or seal and refrigerate for at least 30 minutes, or up to 2 hours, to allow the flavors to meld together.

3) Preheat your grill to medium-high heat.

4) Remove the salmon fillets from the marinade and discard any excess marinade.

5) Place the salmon fillets skin-side down on the preheated grill. Grill for about 4-5 minutes per side or until the salmon is cooked through and flakes easily with a fork.

6) Once cooked, remove the grilled salmon from the grill and transfer to a serving platter.

7) Garnish the grilled salmon with fresh parsley, if desired, and serve with lemon wedges on the side.

NUTRITION
Cal 320; Fat 20 g; Carb 2 g;
Protein 30 g; Fiber: 0 g; Sodium: 130 mg

Mediterranean Baked Cod

Prep time: 10 min	Cook time 15 min	Serving: 2

INGREDIENTS

- *2 cod fillets (about 6 oz each)*
- *2 tablespoons olive oil*
- *Zest of 1 lemon*
- *2 cloves garlic, minced*
- *2 tablespoons chopped fresh parsley*
- *1/2 teaspoon paprika*
- *Salt and black pepper, to taste*
- *Lemon wedges for serving*
- *Fresh parsley for garnish (optional)*

1) Preheat your oven to 400°F (200°C).
2) Pat the cod fillets dry with paper towels and place them on a baking sheet lined with parchment paper or aluminum foil.
3) In a small bowl, combine olive oil, lemon zest, minced garlic, chopped fresh parsley, paprika, salt, and black pepper to make the seasoning mixture.
4) Brush the seasoning mixture over the cod fillets, ensuring they are evenly coated on all sides.
5) Bake the cod fillets in the preheated oven for 12-15 minutes or until the fish is opaque and flakes easily with a fork.
6) Once cooked, remove the baked cod from the oven and transfer to serving plates.
7) Garnish the baked cod with fresh parsley, if desired, and serve with lemon wedges on the side.

NUTRITION

Cal 240; Fat 12 g; Carb 1 g; Protein 30 g; Fiber: 0 g; Sodium: 150 mg

Lemon Garlic Shrimp Skewers

| Prep time: 15 min | Cook time: 5 min | Serving: 2 |

INGREDIENTS

- *12 large shrimp, peeled and deveined*
- *2 tablespoons olive oil*
- *Juice of 1 lemon*
- *2 cloves garlic, minced*
- *1 tablespoon chopped fresh parsley*
- *Salt and black pepper, to taste*
- *Wooden skewers, soaked in water for 30 minutes*
- *Lemon wedges for serving*
- *Fresh parsley for garnish (optional)*

1) In a bowl, whisk together olive oil, lemon juice, minced garlic, chopped fresh parsley, salt, and black pepper to make the marinade.

2) Thread the large shrimp onto the soaked wooden skewers, dividing them evenly among the skewers.

3) Place the shrimp skewers in a shallow dish or resealable plastic bag. Pour the marinade over the shrimp skewers, ensuring they are well coated. Cover or seal and refrigerate for at least 30 minutes, or up to 1 hour, to allow the flavors to meld together.

4) Preheat your grill to medium-high heat.

5) Remove the shrimp skewers from the marinade and discard any excess marinade.

6) Grill the shrimp skewers for about 2-3 minutes per side or until the shrimp are pink and opaque.

7) Once cooked, remove the grilled shrimp skewers from the grill and transfer to a serving platter.

8) Garnish the Lemon Garlic Shrimp Skewers with fresh parsley, if desired, and serve with lemon wedges on the side.

NUTRITION

Cal 180; Fat 10 g; Carb 4 g;
Protein 18 g; Fiber: 0 g; Sodium: 190 mg

Mediterranean Style Seared Tuna

Prep time: 10 min | Cook time: 6 min | Serving: 2

INGREDIENTS

- *2 tuna steaks (about 6 oz each)*
- *1 tablespoon crushed peppercorns*
- *1 teaspoon garlic powder*
- *1 teaspoon dried oregano*
- *Salt, to taste*
- *2 tablespoons olive oil*
- *Lemon wedges for serving*
- *Fresh parsley for garnish (optional)*

1) In a shallow dish, combine crushed peppercorns, garlic powder, dried oregano, and a pinch of salt.

2) Pat the tuna steaks dry with paper towels and coat them evenly in the spice mixture, pressing gently to adhere.

3) Heat olive oil in a large skillet over medium-high heat until shimmering.

4) Carefully place the seasoned tuna steaks in the hot skillet and sear for about 2-3 minutes on each side, depending on thickness or until golden brown on the outside and still pink in the center. For a rare to medium-rare doneness, aim for an internal temperature of about 125-130°F (52-55°C).

5) Once seared to your liking, remove the tuna steaks from the skillet and transfer to serving plates.

6) Garnish the Mediterranean Style Seared Tuna with fresh parsley, if desired, and serve immediately with lemon wedges on the side.

NUTRITION
Cal 280; Fat 15 g; Carb 1 g;
Protein 34 g; Fiber: 0 g; Sodium: 70 mg

Baked Mediterranean Stuffed Sole

Prep time: 20 min	Cook time 20 min	Serving: 2

INGREDIENTS

- *2 sole fillets (about 6 oz each)*
- *1 cup fresh spinach, chopped*
- *1/4 cup sun-dried tomatoes, chopped*
- *1/4 cup black olives, sliced*
- *1/4 cup crumbled feta cheese*
- *2 cloves garlic, minced*
- *1 tablespoon olive oil*
- *Salt and black pepper, to taste*
- *Lemon wedges for serving*
- *Fresh parsley for garnish (optional)*

1) Preheat your oven to 375°F (190°C).
2) In a skillet, heat olive oil over medium heat. Add minced garlic and sauté for 1-2 minutes until fragrant.
3) Add chopped spinach to the skillet and cook until wilted, about 2-3 minutes.
4) Remove the skillet from heat and stir in chopped sun-dried tomatoes, sliced black olives, and crumbled feta cheese. Season with salt and black pepper to taste.
5) Place the sole fillets on a baking sheet lined with parchment paper or aluminum foil.
6) Spoon the spinach mixture evenly onto each sole fillet, pressing gently to pack the filling.
7) Roll up the sole fillets and secure with toothpicks, if needed, to prevent the filling from falling out.
8) Bake the stuffed sole fillets in the preheated oven for 15-20 minutes or until the fish is cooked through and flakes easily with a fork.
9) Once baked, remove the stuffed sole fillets from the oven and transfer to serving plates.
10) Garnish with fresh parsley, if desired, and serve with lemon wedges on the side.

NUTRITION
Cal 290; Fat 16 g; Carb 8 g;
Protein 31 g; Fiber: 3 g; Sodium: 620 mg

Grilled Lemon Garlic Scallops

| Prep time: 15 min | Cook time 5 min | Serving: 2 |

INGREDIENTS

- *12 large scallops*
- *2 tablespoons olive oil*
- *Juice of 1 lemon*
- *2 cloves garlic, minced*
- *1 tablespoon chopped fresh parsley*
- *Salt and black pepper, to taste*
- *Wooden skewers, soaked in water for 30 minutes*
- *Lemon wedges for serving*
- *Fresh parsley for garnish (optional)*

1) In a bowl, whisk together olive oil, lemon juice, minced garlic, chopped fresh parsley, salt, and black pepper to make the marinade.

2) Place the scallops in the marinade, turning to coat them evenly. Cover the bowl and refrigerate for at least 30 minutes, or up to 1 hour, to allow the flavors to meld together.

3) Preheat your grill to medium-high heat.

4) Remove the scallops from the marinade and discard any excess mar-inade.

5) Thread the scallops onto the soaked wooden skewers, dividing them evenly among the skewers.

6) Grill the scallop skewers for about 2-3 minutes per side or until the scallops are opaque and cooked through.

7) Once cooked, remove the grilled scallop skewers from the grill and transfer to a serving platter.

8) Garnish the Grilled Lemon Garlic Scallops with fresh parsley, if desired, and serve with lemon wedges on the side.

NUTRITION

Cal 200; Fat 8 g; Carb 4 g;
Protein 22 g; Fiber: 0 g; Sodium: 350 mg

Mediterranean Style Baked Red Snapper

Prep time: 15 min | Cook time: 20 min | Serving: 2

INGREDIENTS

- *2 red snapper fillets (about 6 oz each)*
- *1 cup diced tomatoes (fresh or canned)*
- *1/4 cup black olives, sliced*
- *2 tablespoons capers, drained*
- *2 cloves garlic, minced*
- *2 tablespoons olive oil*
- *Salt and black pepper, to taste*
- *Lemon wedges for serving*
- *Fresh parsley for garnish (optional)*

1) Preheat your oven to 375°F (190°C).

2) Pat the red snapper fillets dry with paper towels and place them in a baking dish lined with parchment paper or aluminum foil.

3) In a bowl, combine diced tomatoes, sliced black olives, drained capers, minced garlic, and olive oil. Season the mixture with salt and black pepper to taste.

4) Spoon the tomato mixture over the red snapper fillets, dividing it evenly among them.

5) Bake the red snapper fillets in the preheated oven for 15-20 minutes or until the fish is tender and flakes easily with a fork.

6) Once cooked, remove the baked red snapper from the oven and transfer to serving plates.

7) Garnish with fresh parsley, if desired, and serve with lemon wedges on the side.

NUTRITION

Cal 280; Fat 14 g; Carb 4 g;
Protein 34 g; Fiber: 1 g; Sodium: 700 mg

Shrimp and Vegetable Stir-Fry

| Prep time: 15 min | Cook time 10 min | Serving: 2 |

INGREDIENTS

- *12 large shrimp, peeled and deveined*
- *1 cup bell peppers, thinly sliced (assorted colors)*
- *1 cup broccoli florets*
- *1 cup snap peas, trimmed*
- *2 cloves garlic, minced*
- *2 tablespoons olive oil*
- *1 teaspoon dried oregano*
- *1/2 teaspoon dried basil*
- *Salt and black pepper, to taste*
- *Red pepper flakes, optional (for added heat)*
- *Lemon wedges for serving*
- *Fresh parsley for garnish (optional)*

1) Heat olive oil in a large skillet or wok over medium-high heat.
2) Add minced garlic to the skillet and sauté until fragrant, about 1 minute.
3) Add bell peppers, broccoli florets, and snap peas to the skillet. Stir-fry for 3-4 minutes or until the vegetables are tender-crisp.
4) Push the vegetables to one side of the skillet and add the shrimp to the empty space. Cook the shrimp for 2-3 minutes on each side or until they turn pink and opaque.
5) Season the shrimp and vegetables with dried oregano, dried basil, salt, black pepper, and red pepper flakes (if using). Toss everything together until well combined.
6) Once cooked, remove the shrimp and vegetable stir-fry from the heat and transfer to serving plates.
7) Garnish with fresh parsley, if desired, and serve immediately with lemon wedges on the side.

NUTRITION
Cal 250; Fat 14 g; Carb 16 g;
Protein 18 g; Fiber: 6 g; Sodium: 250 mg

Lemon Herb Baked Salmon Patties

| Prep time: 15 min | Cook time 20 min | Serving: 2 |

INGREDIENTS

- *1 can (14.75 oz) canned salmon, drained and flaked*
- *1/4 cup almond flour*
- *Zest of 1 lemon*
- *2 tablespoons chopped fresh herbs (such as parsley, dill, or chives)*
- *1 large egg, beaten*
- *1 tablespoon olive oil*
- *Salt and black pepper, to taste*
- *Lemon wedges for serving*
- *Fresh herbs for garnish (optional)*

1) Preheat your oven to 375°F (190°C). Line a baking sheet with parchment paper or lightly grease it with olive oil.

2) In a large mixing bowl, combine the canned salmon, almond flour, lemon zest, chopped fresh herbs, beaten egg, olive oil, salt, and black pepper. Mix until well combined.

3) Divide the salmon mixture into 4 equal portions and shape each portion into a patty.

4) Place the salmon patties on the prepared baking sheet.

5) Bake the salmon patties in the preheated oven for 15-20 minutes or until they are golden brown and crispy on the outside and cooked through.

6) Once cooked, remove the salmon patties from the oven and transfer to serving plates.

7) Garnish with fresh herbs, if desired, and serve with lemon wedges on the side.

NUTRITION

Cal 300; Fat 18 g; Carb 6 g; Protein 24 g; Fiber: 2 g; Sodium: 500 mg

Mediterranean Style Steamed Mussels

Prep time: 10 min	Cook time 10 min	Serving: 2

INGREDIENTS

- *2 pounds fresh mussels, cleaned and debearded*
- *1 tablespoon olive oil*
- *3 cloves garlic, minced*
- *1/2 cup dry white wine*
- *1/2 cup diced tomatoes (fresh or canned)*
- *2 tablespoons chopped fresh parsley*
- *1 tablespoon chopped fresh basil*
- *Salt and black pepper, to taste*
- *Crushed red pepper flakes, optional (for added heat)*
- *Crusty whole-grain bread for serving*

1) Heat olive oil in a large pot or Dutch oven over medium heat. Add minced garlic and sauté until fragrant, about 1 minute.

2) Pour in the white wine and bring it to a simmer.

3) Add the diced tomatoes, chopped fresh parsley, and chopped fresh basil to the pot. Season with salt, black pepper, and crushed red pepper flakes (if using). Stir to combine.

4) Increase the heat to medium-high and bring the broth to a boil.

5) Once the broth is boiling, add the cleaned mussels to the pot. Cover with a lid and steam for 5-7 minutes or until the mussels have opened. Discard any mussels that do not open.

6) Once cooked, remove the pot from the heat.

7) Ladle the Mediterranean Style Steamed Mussels into serving bowls, making sure to distribute the broth evenly.

NUTRITION
Cal 300; Fat 8 g; Carb 18 g;
Protein 24 g; Fiber: 3 g; Sodium: 600 mg

Salmon with White Sauce

Prep time: 10 min	Cook time 15 min	Serving: 2

INGREDIENTS

- *2 salmon fillets (6-8 ounces each)*
- *Salt and black pepper, to taste*
- *1 tablespoon olive oil*
- *2 cloves garlic, minced*
- *1/2 cup dry white wine*
- *1/2 cup chicken or vegetable broth*
- *1/2 cup heavy cream*
- *1 tablespoon Dijon mustard*
- *2 tablespoons chopped fresh parsley*
- *Lemon wedges, for serving*

1) Season the salmon fillets with salt and black pepper on both sides.

2) Heat olive oil in a skillet over medium-high heat. Once hot, add the salmon fillets to the skillet, skin side down. Cook for about 4-5 minutes until the skin is crispy and golden brown.

3) Flip the salmon fillets and add minced garlic to the skillet. Cook for an additional 2 minutes until the garlic is fragrant.

4) Pour white wine into the skillet, scraping up any browned bits from the bottom of the pan. Allow the wine to simmer for a few minutes to reduce slightly.

5) Stir in chicken or vegetable broth and bring the mixture to a simmer.

6) Reduce the heat to medium-low and stir in heavy cream and Dijon mustard. Simmer for another 3-4 minutes until the sauce thickens slightly.

7) Return the salmon fillets to the skillet, spooning the sauce over them. Cook for an additional 2-3 minutes until the salmon is cooked through and flakes easily with a fork.

8) Sprinkle chopped fresh parsley over the salmon.

9) Serve the Salmon with White Sauce hot, with lemon wedges on the side for squeezing over the salmon.

NUTRITION

Cal 350; Fat 20 g; Carb 5 g;
Protein 30 g; Fiber: 1 g; Sodium: 580 mg

Clams Toscano

| | Prep time: 10 min | | Cook time 15 min | | Serving: 2 |

INGREDIENTS

- *1 pound fresh clams, cleaned*
- *2 tablespoons olive oil*
- *3 cloves garlic, minced*
- *1/4 teaspoon red pepper flakes (adjust to taste)*
- *1/2 cup dry white wine*
- *1/2 cup cherry tomatoes, halved*
- *2 tablespoons chopped fresh parsley*
- *Salt and black pepper, to taste*
- *Crusty bread for serving*

1) In a large skillet, heat olive oil over medium heat. Add minced gar-lic and red pepper flakes. Sauté for 1-2 minutes until fragrant.
2) Add the cleaned clams to the skillet and toss to coat them in the gar-lic and oil mixture.
3) Pour in the dry white wine and cover the skillet. Allow the clams to cook for 5-7 minutes or until they have opened up. Discard any clams that do not open.
4) Once the clams have opened, add the cherry tomatoes to the skillet. Cook for another 1-2 minutes until the tomatoes have softened slightly.
5) Season the clams Toscano with salt and black pepper to taste. Sprin-kle chopped fresh parsley over the top.
6) Serve the Clams Toscano hot, with crusty bread for dipping and soaking up the delicious broth.

NUTRITION
Cal 250; Fat 12 g; Carb 12 g;
Protein 20 g; Fiber: 1 g; Sodium: 650 mg

Greek Stuffed Squid

| Prep time: 20 min | Cook time 30 min | Serving: 2 |

INGREDIENTS

- 8 medium squid bodies, cleaned
- 3 tablespoons golden raisins
- 3 tablespoons pine nuts, toasted
- 1/4 cup red wine
- 1/4 cup plain dried breadcrumbs
- 1/2 cup tomato sauce
- 1 garlic clove, minced
- 1 teaspoon dried mint
- 1 tablespoon extra-virgin olive oil
- 1 onion, finely chopped
- 2 anchovy fillets, rinsed, and minced
- 2 tablespoons fresh parsley, minced
- Salt and pepper, to taste

1) Preheat the oven to 375°F (190°C).
2) In a small bowl, soak the golden raisins in red wine for 10 minutes.
3) In another bowl, mix together the breadcrumbs, tomato sauce, minced garlic, and dried mint.
4) Add the soaked golden raisins (along with any remaining wine) and toasted pine nuts to the breadcrumb mixture. Stir well to combine.
5) Stuff the cleaned squid bodies with the breadcrumb mixture, leaving some room at the top for expansion.
6) In a skillet, heat the olive oil over medium heat. Add the chopped onion and minced anchovy fillets. Cook until the onions are soft and translucent, about 5 minutes.
7) Stir in the minced tentacles and cook for another 2-3 minutes.
8) Remove the skillet from heat and stir in the fresh parsley. Season with salt and pepper to taste.
9) Stuff the cooked onion and tentacle mixture into the stuffed squid bodies, packing it tightly.
10) Place the stuffed squid in a baking dish and cover with foil.

11) Bake in the preheated oven for 20-25 minutes or until the squid is tender and the filling is heated through.

12) Serve the Greek Stuffed Squid hot, garnished with additional parsley if desired.

NUTRITION
Cal 450; Fat 20 g; Carb 45 g; Protein 25 g; Fiber: 4 g; Sodium: 600 mg

Calamari Stew

| Prep time: 15 min | Cook time 30 min | Serving: 2 |

INGREDIENTS

- *1 pound small squid, bodies sliced crosswise into 1-inch-thick rings, tentacles halved*
- *1 (14.5-ounce) can whole peeled tomatoes, drained and chopped coarsely*
- *2 tablespoons extra-virgin olive oil, plus extra for serving*
- *1/8 teaspoon red pepper flakes*
- *2 tablespoons pitted brine-cured green olives, coarsely chopped*
- *1/4 cup red wine*
- *1/2 tablespoon capers, rinsed*
- *1 celery rib, thinly sliced*
- *1/2 onion, finely chopped*
- *1 1/2 tablespoons fresh parsley, minced*
- *4 garlic cloves, minced*
- *Salt and pepper, to taste*

1) In a large pot, heat 2 tablespoons of olive oil over medium heat. Add the red pepper flakes and cook for 1 minute until fragrant.

2) Add the chopped olives, red wine, capers, celery, and onion to the pot. Cook for about 5 minutes, stirring occasionally until the vegetables are softened.

3) Add the sliced squid rings and halved tentacles to the pot. Cook for another 5 minutes, stirring occasionally until the squid is opaque and just cooked through.

4) Stir in the chopped tomatoes and minced garlic. Bring the mixture to a simmer.

5) Reduce the heat to low, cover, and let the stew simmer for 15-20 minutes, stirring occasionally, to allow the flavors to meld together.

6) Season the stew with salt and pepper to taste.

7) Serve the Classic Calamari Stew hot, garnished with minced parsley and a drizzle of extra-virgin olive oil.

NUTRITION

Cal 480; Fat 20 g; Carb 40 g;
Protein 30 g; Fiber: 8 g; Sodium: 800 mg

Octopus Braised in Red Wine

Prep time: 15 min
Cook time: 1 hour 30 min
Serving: 2

INGREDIENTS

- *1 pound (450g) octopus, cleaned, and tentacles separated*
- *2 cups dry red wine*
- *2 cups water*
- *1 onion, thinly sliced*
- *4 cloves garlic, minced*
- *2 bay leaves*
- *1 teaspoon dried oregano*
- *1 teaspoon dried thyme*
- *1/2 teaspoon red pepper flakes*
- *Salt and black pepper, to taste*
- *2 tablespoons extra-virgin olive oil*
- *Fresh parsley, chopped for garnish*
- *Lemon wedges for serving*

1) In a large pot, combine the octopus, red wine, water, sliced onion, minced garlic, bay leaves, dried oregano, dried thyme, red pepper flakes, salt, and black pepper.

2) Bring the mixture to a boil over high heat. Once boiling, reduce the heat to low, cover, and let the octopus simmer for 1 hour to 1 hour 15 minutes or until tender. The octopus should be easily pierced with a fork.

3) Preheat your grill to medium-high heat.

4) Remove the octopus from the pot and pat dry with paper towels. Discard the cooking liquid and aromatics.

5) Brush the octopus with olive oil on both sides.

6) Place the octopus on the preheated grill and cook for 3-4 minutes on each side until charred and crispy.

7) Transfer the grilled octopus to a serving platter. Garnish with chopped fresh parsley and serve hot with lemon wedges on the side.

NUTRITION

Cal 380; Fat 15 g; Carb 10 g;
Protein 45 g; Fiber: 1 g; Sodium: 520 mg

Octopus in Honey Sauce

Prep time: 15 min | Cook time 1 hour 30 min | Serving: 2

INGREDIENTS

- *1 pound (450g) octopus, cleaned, and tentacles separated*
- *4 cups water*
- *1 onion, quartered*
- *2 cloves garlic, smashed*
- *2 bay leaves*
- *1/4 cup honey*
- *2 tablespoons balsamic vinegar*
- *2 tablespoons soy sauce*
- *1 tablespoon olive oil*
- *1 teaspoon dried oregano*
- *1/2 teaspoon red pepper flakes (optional)*
- *Salt and black pepper, to taste*
- *Fresh parsley, chopped for garnish*
- *Lemon wedges for serving*

1) In a large pot, combine the octopus, water, quartered onion, smashed garlic cloves, and bay leaves.

2) Bring the mixture to a boil over high heat. Once boiling, reduce the heat to low, cover, and let the octopus simmer for 1 hour to 1 hour 15 minutes or until tender. The octopus should be easily pierced with a fork.

3) While the octopus is cooking, prepare the honey sauce. In a small bowl, whisk together the honey, balsamic vinegar, soy sauce, olive oil, dried oregano, red pepper flakes (if using), salt, and black pepper.

4) Once the octopus is tender, remove it from the pot and pat dry with paper towels.

5) Preheat your grill to medium-high heat.

6) Brush the octopus with the prepared honey sauce on all sides.

7) Place the octopus on the preheated grill and cook for 3-4 minutes on each side until charred and caramelized.

8) Transfer the grilled octopus to a serving platter. Drizzle with any remaining honey sauce and garnish with chopped fresh parsley.

9) Serve hot with lemon wedges on the side.

NUTRITION

Cal 320; Fat 10 g; Carb 25 g;
Protein 35 g; Fiber: 1 g; Sodium: 520 mg

Mahi-Mahi and Mushrooms

| Prep time: 15 min | Cook time 20 min | Serving: 2 |

INGREDIENTS

- *2 Mahi-Mahi fillets (6-8 ounces each)*
- *Salt and black pepper, to taste*
- *2 tablespoons olive oil, divided*
- *8 ounces portobello mushrooms, sliced*
- *2 cloves garlic, minced*
- *1/4 cup white wine*
- *2 tablespoons lemon juice*
- *1 tablespoon chopped fresh parsley*
- *Lemon wedges for serving*

1) Season the Mahi-Mahi fillets with salt and black pepper on both sides.
2) In a large skillet, heat 1 tablespoon of olive oil over medium-high heat. Add the Mahi-Mahi fillets to the skillet and cook for about 3-4 minutes on each side or until golden brown and cooked through. Remove the fillets from the skillet and set aside.
3) In the same skillet, add the remaining tablespoon of olive oil. Add the sliced mushrooms and minced garlic to the skillet. Cook for about 5 minutes or until the mushrooms are golden brown and tender.
4) Pour white wine and lemon juice into the skillet, scraping up any browned bits from the bottom of the pan. Allow the mixture to simmer for 2-3 minutes to reduce slightly.
5) Return the Mahi-Mahi fillets to the skillet, spooning the mushroom mixture over the top. Cook for another 2-3 minutes or until the fish is heated through.
6) Sprinkle chopped fresh parsley over the Mahi-Mahi and mushrooms.
7) Serve the Mahi-Mahi and Mushrooms hot, with lemon wedges on the side for squeezing over the fish.

NUTRITION
Cal 320; Fat 15 g; Carb 10 g; Protein 35 g; Fiber: 3 g; Sodium: 580 mg

Shrimp and Feta Saganaki

| Prep time: 10 min | Cook time 15 min | Serving: 2 |

INGREDIENTS

- 1 tablespoon olive oil
- 1 small onion, finely chopped
- 2 cloves garlic, minced
- 1/2 teaspoon red pepper flakes (adjust to taste)
- 1 (14.5-ounce) can diced tomatoes
- 1/4 cup dry white wine
- 8 ounces large shrimp, peeled and deveined
- 1/4 cup crumbled feta cheese
- 1 tablespoon chopped fresh parsley
- Salt and black pepper, to taste
- Crusty bread, for serving

1) Heat olive oil in a skillet over medium heat. Add the chopped onion and cook for 3-4 minutes until softened.
2) Add minced garlic and red pepper flakes to the skillet. Cook for another 1-2 minutes until fragrant.
3) Stir in the diced tomatoes (with their juices) and white wine. Allow the mixture to simmer for about 5 minutes to thicken slightly.
4) Add the peeled and deveined shrimp to the skillet. Cook for 3-4 minutes until the shrimp are pink and cooked through.
5) Season the shrimp and tomato mixture with salt and black pepper to taste.
6) Sprinkle crumbled feta cheese over the top of the shrimp mixture. Cover the skillet and let it cook for another 1-2 minutes until the cheese is slightly melted.
7) Garnish with chopped fresh parsley.
8) Serve the Shrimp and Feta Saganaki hot, with crusty bread for dip-ping.

NUTRITION

Cal 320; Fat 20 g; Carb 10 g; Protein 25 g; Fiber: 2 g; Sodium: 820 mg

Herb-Crumbed Fish Saganaki

Prep time: 15 min | Cook time: 20 min | Serving: 2

INGREDIENTS

- *2 fish fillets (such as cod, haddock, or tilapia), about 6-8 ounces each*
- *Salt and black pepper, to taste*
- *2 tablespoons olive oil, divided*
- *2 cloves garlic, minced*
- *1 small onion, finely chopped*
- *1 (14.5-ounce) can diced tomatoes*
- *1/4 cup dry white wine*
- *1/4 cup crumbled feta cheese*
- *1/4 cup breadcrumbs*
- *1 tablespoon chopped fresh parsley*
- *1 teaspoon dried oregano*
- *1/2 teaspoon dried thyme*
- *Lemon wedges, for serving*

1) Preheat your oven to 375°F (190°C).
2) Season the fish fillets with salt and black pepper on both sides.
3) In a skillet, heat 1 tablespoon of olive oil over medium-high heat. Add the fish fillets to the skillet and cook for about 2-3 minutes on each side until lightly browned. Remove the fish from the skillet and set aside.
4) In the same skillet, add the remaining tablespoon of olive oil. Add minced garlic and chopped onion to the skillet. Cook for 3-4 minutes until softened and fragrant.
5) Stir in the diced tomatoes (with their juices) and white wine. Allow the mixture to simmer for about 5 minutes to thicken slightly.
6) Return the fish fillets to the skillet, nestling them into the tomato mixture.
7) In a small bowl, mix together the breadcrumbs, crumbled feta cheese, chopped parsley, dried oregano, and dried thyme.
8) Sprinkle the breadcrumb mixture over the top of the fish fillets in the skillet.
9) Transfer the skillet to the preheated oven and bake for 12-15 minutes until the fish is cooked through and the breadcrumbs are golden brown and crispy.
10) Serve the Herb-Crumbed Fish Saganaki hot, with lemon wedges on the side for squeezing over the fish.

NUTRITION

Cal 350; Fat 15 g; Carb 15 g;
Protein 30 g; Fiber: 2 g; Sodium: 600 mg

Mediterranean Fish Kebabs

Prep time: 15 min	Cook time: 10 min	Serving: 2

INGREDIENTS

- *2 fish fillets (such as salmon, cod, or halibut), about 6 ounces each, cut into cubes*
- *1 small red onion, cut into chunks*
- *1 bell pepper (any color), cut into chunks*
- *8 cherry tomatoes*
- *8 small mushrooms*
- *2 tablespoons olive oil*
- *2 cloves garlic, minced*
- *1 teaspoon dried oregano*
- *1 teaspoon dried thyme*
- *Salt and black pepper, to taste*
- *Lemon wedges for serving*
- *Metal or wooden skewers, soaked in water if wooden*

1) Preheat your grill to medium-high heat.
2) In a small bowl, mix together the olive oil, minced garlic, dried oregano, dried thyme, salt, and black pepper.
3) Thread the fish cubes, red onion chunks, bell pepper chunks, cherry tomatoes, and mushrooms onto the skewers, alternating the ingredients.
4) Brush the skewers with the olive oil mixture on all sides.
5) Place the skewers on the preheated grill. Cook for about 4-5 minutes on each side or until the fish is cooked through and the vegetables are tender and slightly charred.
6) Remove the skewers from the grill and transfer them to a serving platter.
7) Serve the Mediterranean Fish Kebabs hot, with lemon wedges on the side for squeezing over the kebabs.

NUTRITION

Cal 280; Fat 12 g; Carb 10 g;
Protein 30 g; Fiber: 2 g; Sodium: 650 mg

HEALTHY VEGETARIAN & VEGAN RECIPES

Zucchini Noodles with Pesto

Prep time: 15 min | Cook time 0 min | Serving: 2

INGREDIENTS

- *For the zucchini noodles:*
- *2 medium zucchini, spiralized into noodles*
- *1 cup cherry tomatoes, halved*
- *1/4 cup sliced olives (Kalamata or black)*
- *For the pesto:*
- *2 cups fresh basil leaves*
- *2 cloves garlic*
- *1/4 cup pine nuts*
- *1/4 cup grated Parmesan cheese*
- *1/4 cup extra virgin olive oil*
- *Salt and black pepper, to taste*

For the pesto:

1) In a food processor, combine the fresh basil leaves, garlic cloves, pine nuts, and grated Parmesan cheese.
2) Pulse until the ingredients are finely chopped.
3) With the food processor running, gradually drizzle in the olive oil until the pesto reaches your desired consistency. You may need to scrape down the sides of the food processor with a spatula to ensure all ingredients are well combined.
4) Season the pesto with salt and black pepper to taste. Set aside.

For the zucchini noodles:

5) Spiralize the zucchini into noodles using a spiralizer.
6) In a large mixing bowl, toss the zucchini noodles with the homemade pesto until evenly coated.
7) Add the halved cherry tomatoes and sliced olives to the bowl and gently toss to combine.

To serve:

8) Divide the zucchini noodles with pesto between two plates.
9) Garnish with additional grated Parmesan cheese and fresh basil leaves, if desired.

NUTRITION

Cal 350; Fat 32 g; Carb 12 g; Protein 10 g; Fiber: 5 g; Sodium: 300 mg

Mushroom and Spinach Stuffed Portobello Mushrooms

| Prep time: 15 min | Cook time 20 min | Serving: 2 |

INGREDIENTS

- *2 large portobello mushrooms*
- *1 tablespoon olive oil*
- *1 cup mushrooms, diced*
- *2 cups fresh spinach, chopped*
- *2 cloves garlic, minced*
- *1/4 cup almond flour (or breadcrumbs for traditional version)*
- *1/4 cup grated Parmesan cheese*
- *Salt and black pepper, to taste*
- *Fresh parsley, chopped for garnish (optional)*

1) Preheat your oven to 375°F (190°C).
2) Clean the portobello mushrooms and remove the stems. Use a spoon to gently scrape out the gills from the underside of the mushrooms to create more room for stuffing.
3) In a skillet, heat olive oil over medium heat. Add diced mushrooms and sauté until they release their moisture and become tender, about 5 minutes.
4) Add chopped spinach and minced garlic to the skillet. Cook until the spinach is wilted and the garlic is fragrant, about 2-3 minutes.
5) Remove the skillet from heat and stir in almond flour (or breadcrumbs) and grated Parmesan cheese. Season with salt and black pepper to taste.
6) Divide the mushroom and spinach mixture evenly among the hol-lowed-out portobello mushroom caps, pressing gently to pack the filling.
7) Place the stuffed portobello mushrooms on a baking sheet lined with parchment paper or aluminum foil.
8) Bake in the preheated oven for 15-20 minutes or until the mush-rooms are tender and the filling is golden brown.
9) Remove from the oven and garnish with chopped fresh parsley, if desired, before serving.

NUTRITION
Cal 180; Fat 12 g; Carb 10 g;
Protein 10 g; Fiber: 4 g; Sodium: 280 mg

Cauliflower Rice Bowl

| Prep time: 10 min | Cook time 15 min | Serving: 2 |

INGREDIENTS

- *1 small head cauliflower, riced (or 4 cups pre-riced cauliflower)*
- *1 tablespoon olive oil*
- *2 cloves garlic, minced*
- *1 can (14 ounces) diced tomatoes, drained*
- *1 can (14 ounces) chickpeas, drained, and rinsed*
- *1/4 cup sliced olives (Kalamata or black)*
- *1/4 cup chopped artichoke hearts*
- *2 cups fresh spinach leaves*
- *1 teaspoon dried oregano*
- *1/2 teaspoon garlic powder*
- *Salt and black pepper, to taste*

1) If using a whole cauliflower head, remove the leaves and stem, then chop the cauliflower into florets. Working in batches, pulse the cauliflower florets in a food processor until they resemble rice grains.
2) In a large skillet, heat olive oil over medium heat. Add minced garlic and sauté for 1-2 minutes until fragrant.
3) Add the riced cauliflower to the skillet and cook for 5-6 minutes, stirring occasionally until it begins to soften.
4) Stir in the drained diced tomatoes, chickpeas, sliced olives, and chopped artichoke hearts. Cook for an additional 3-4 minutes, allowing the flavors to meld.
5) Add fresh spinach leaves to the skillet and cook for 1-2 minutes until wilted.
6) Season the cauliflower rice mixture with dried oregano, garlic powder, salt, and black pepper. Stir to combine.
7) Once everything is heated through and well combined, remove the skillet from heat.
8) Divide the Mediterranean Cauliflower Rice Bowl between two bowls.

NUTRITION
Cal 320; Fat 10 g; Carb 46 g;
Protein 14 g; Fiber: 14 g; Sodium: 750 mg

Vegetable Ratatouille

| Prep time: 15 min | Cook time 30 min | Serving: 2 |

INGREDIENTS

- *1 medium eggplant, diced*
- *1 zucchini, diced*
- *1 yellow bell pepper, diced*
- *1 red bell pepper, diced*
- *1 onion, diced*
- *2 tomatoes, diced*
- *3 cloves garlic, minced*
- *2 tablespoons olive oil*
- *1 teaspoon dried thyme*
- *1 teaspoon dried oregano*
- *Salt and black pepper, to taste*
- *Fresh basil leaves, chopped, for garnish (optional)*

1) Heat olive oil in a large skillet over medium heat. Add minced garlic and sauté for about 1 minute until fragrant.
2) Add diced eggplant, zucchini, bell peppers, and onion to the skillet. Cook, stirring occasionally, for about 10 minutes until the vegetables start to soften.
3) Add diced tomatoes, dried thyme, dried oregano, salt, and black pepper to the skillet. Stir well to combine.
4) Reduce the heat to low, cover the skillet, and let the ratatouille simmer for about 15-20 minutes, stirring occasionally until all the vegetables are tender and the flavors have melded.
5) Taste and adjust seasoning if needed.
6) Once the ratatouille is ready, remove it from heat.

NUTRITION
Cal 220; Fat 11 g; Carb 30 g;
Protein 5 g; Fiber: 9 g; Sodium: 20 mg

Mediterranean Veggie Stir-Fry

| Prep time: 10 min | Cook time 10 min | Serving: 2 |

INGREDIENTS

- *1 bell pepper, thinly sliced*
- *1 zucchini, thinly sliced*
- *1 small eggplant, diced*
- *1 cup cherry tomatoes, halved*
- *1/2 red onion, thinly sliced*
- *2 tablespoons olive oil*
- *2 cloves garlic, minced*
- *1 teaspoon dried Italian herbs (such as basil, oregano, thyme)*
- *Salt and black pepper, to taste*
- *Fresh parsley, chopped, for garnish (optional)*
- *Cauliflower rice or whole-grain couscous, for serving*

1) Heat olive oil in a large skillet or wok over medium-high heat.
2) Add minced garlic to the skillet and sauté for about 30 seconds until fragrant.
3) Add sliced bell pepper, zucchini, diced eggplant, cherry tomatoes, and sliced red onion to the skillet.
4) Stir-fry the vegetables for about 5-7 minutes until they are tender-crisp and lightly charred.
5) Sprinkle dried Italian herbs over the vegetables and season with salt and black pepper to taste. Stir well to combine.
6) Once the vegetables are cooked to your liking, remove the skillet from heat.
7) Serve the Mediterranean Veggie Stir-Fry hot over cauliflower rice or whole-grain couscous.
8) Garnish with chopped fresh parsley if desired.

NUTRITION
Cal 150; Fat 10 g; Carb 15 g;
Protein 3 g; Fiber: 5 g; Sodium: 15 mg

Spaghetti Squash with Tomato Basil Sauce

| Prep time: 10 min | Cook time 45 min | Serving: 2 |

INGREDIENTS

- *1 medium spaghetti squash*
- *2 tablespoons olive oil*
- *Salt and black pepper, to taste*
- *2 cups homemade tomato basil sauce (see recipe below)*
- *Grated Parmesan cheese, for serving*
- *Fresh basil leaves, chopped, for garnish (optional)*
- **For the homemade tomato basil sauce:**
- *2 tablespoons olive oil*
- *2 cloves garlic, minced*
- *1 can (14 ounces) diced tomatoes*
- *1/4 cup tomato paste*
- *1 teaspoon dried basil*
- *Salt and black pepper, to taste*

For the spaghetti squash:

1) Preheat your oven to 400°F (200°C).
2) Cut the spaghetti squash in half lengthwise and scoop out the seeds.
3) Drizzle the cut sides of the squash with olive oil and season with salt and black pepper.
4) Place the squash halves cut side down on a baking sheet lined with parchment paper or aluminum foil.
5) Roast in the preheated oven for 40-45 minutes or until the squash is tender and easily pierced with a fork.
6) Remove the squash from the oven and let it cool slightly.
7) Use a fork to scrape the flesh of the squash into strands.

For the homemade tomato basil sauce:

8) In a saucepan, heat olive oil over medium heat.
9) Add minced garlic to the saucepan and sauté for about 1 minute until fragrant.
10) Add diced tomatoes (with their juices) and tomato paste to the saucepan.
11) Stir in dried basil, salt, and black pepper to taste.
12) Simmer the sauce for about 15-20 minutes, stirring occasionally until it thickens slightly.

To assemble:

13) Divide the spaghetti squash strands between two plates.
14) Spoon homemade tomato basil sauce over the spaghetti squash.
15) Sprinkle grated Parmesan cheese over the top.
16) Garnish with chopped fresh basil leaves if desired.

NUTRITION
Cal 250; Fat 14 g; Carb 28 g;
Protein 5 g; Fiber: 6 g; Sodium: 450 mg

Eggplant Caponata

Prep time: 15 min | Cook time: 25 min | Serving: 2

INGREDIENTS

- *1 large eggplant, diced*
- *2 tomatoes, diced*
- *1 onion, diced*
- *2 celery stalks, diced*
- *2 tablespoons capers, drained*
- *3 cloves garlic, minced*
- *3 tablespoons olive oil*
- *2 tablespoons red wine vinegar*
- *1 tablespoon tomato paste*
- *1 teaspoon sugar (optional)*
- *Salt and black pepper, to taste*
- *Fresh basil leaves, chopped, for garnish (optional)*

1) Heat olive oil in a large skillet over medium heat.
2) Add minced garlic to the skillet and sauté for about 1 minute until fragrant.
3) Add diced eggplant, onion, and celery to the skillet. Cook, stirring occasionally, for about 10 minutes until the vegetables start to soften.
4) Stir in diced tomatoes and capers. Cook for an additional 5-7 minutes until the tomatoes release their juices and the vegetables are tender.
5) In a small bowl, mix together red wine vinegar, tomato paste, and sugar (if using) until well combined.
6) Pour the vinegar mixture over the cooked vegetables in the skillet. Stir well to combine.
7) Season the eggplant caponata with salt and black pepper to taste.
8) Continue to cook the caponata for another 3-5 minutes, stirring occasionally until the flavors meld together and the sauce thickens slightly.
9) Once the caponata is ready, remove it from heat.
10) Serve the Eggplant Caponata hot or at room temperature, garnished with chopped fresh basil leaves if desired.

NUTRITION

Cal 250; Fat 14 g; Carb 30 g;
Protein 4 g; Fiber: 9 g; Sodium: 450 mg

Cauliflower and Chickpea Curry

Prep time: 10 min	Cook time 25 min	Serving: 2

INGREDIENTS

- *1 small cauliflower, cut into florets*
- *1 can (14 ounces) chickpeas, drained and rinsed*
- *1 tablespoon coconut oil*
- *2 cloves garlic, minced*
- *1 teaspoon fresh ginger, grated*
- *2 tablespoons tomato paste*
- *1 can (14 ounces) coconut milk*
- *1 tablespoon curry powder*
- *1 teaspoon ground turmeric*
- *1/2 teaspoon ground cumin*
- *1/2 teaspoon ground coriander*
- *Salt and black pepper, to taste*
- *Fresh cilantro leaves, chopped, for garnish (optional)*
- *Cooked brown rice or cauliflower rice, for serving*

1) In a large skillet or pan, heat coconut oil over medium heat.
2) Add minced garlic and grated ginger to the skillet. Sauté for about 1 minute until fragrant.
3) Add cauliflower florets to the skillet and cook for 5-7 minutes until they start to soften and brown slightly.
4) Stir in chickpeas, tomato paste, curry powder, ground turmeric, ground cumin, and ground coriander. Mix well to coat the cauli-flower and chickpeas with the spices.
5) Pour coconut milk into the skillet and stir to combine. Bring the mixture to a simmer.
6) Reduce the heat to low and let the curry simmer for about 10-15 minutes, stirring occasionally until the cauliflower is tender and the sauce has thickened slightly.
7) Season the cauliflower and chickpea curry with salt and black pepper to taste.
8) Once the curry is ready, remove it from heat.
9) Serve the Cauliflower and Chickpea Curry hot over cooked brown rice or cauliflower rice.
10) Garnish with chopped fresh cilantro leaves if desired.

NUTRITION
Cal 380; Fat 28 g; Carb 30 g; Protein 10 g; Fiber: 10 g; Sodium: 270 mg

Balsamic Roasted Green Beans

| Prep time: 10 min | Cook time: 15 min | Serving: 2 |

INGREDIENTS

- *1/2 pound green beans, trimmed*
- *1 garlic clove, chopped*
- *1/2 tablespoon balsamic vinegar*
- *1/2 tablespoon olive oil*
- *1/16 teaspoon salt (a pinch)*
- *1/16 teaspoon pepper (a pinch)*

1) Preheat your oven to 425°F (220°C). Line a baking sheet with parchment paper or aluminum foil.

2) In a bowl, toss the trimmed green beans with chopped garlic, bal-samic vinegar, olive oil, salt, and pepper until evenly coated.

3) Spread the green beans out in a single layer on the prepared baking sheet.

4) Roast in the preheated oven for 12-15 minutes or until the green beans are tender and slightly caramelized, stirring halfway through the cooking time.

5) Remove from the oven and serve the Balsamic Roasted Green Beans hot as a delicious side dish.

NUTRITION
Cal 90; Fat 5 g; Carb 11 g;
Protein 2 g; Fiber: 4 g; Sodium: 160 mg

Sautéed Kale

| Prep time: 5 min | Cook time 10 min | Serving: 2 |

INGREDIENTS

- *1 bunch kale (about 8 ounces), stems removed and leaves chopped*
- *2 tablespoons olive oil*
- *2 cloves garlic, minced*
- *1/4 cup chopped red onion*
- *1/4 cup chopped sun-dried tomatoes*
- *1/4 teaspoon red pepper flakes (adjust to taste)*
- *Salt and black pepper, to taste*
- *Lemon wedges, for serving (optional)*

1) Heat olive oil in a large skillet over medium heat.
2) Add minced garlic and chopped red onion to the skillet. Sauté for 2-3 minutes until softened and fragrant.
3) Add chopped sun-dried tomatoes and red pepper flakes to the skillet. Cook for another 1-2 minutes.
4) Increase the heat to medium-high and add the chopped kale leaves to the skillet. Stir well to combine with the other ingredients.
5) Sauté the kale for 5-7 minutes, stirring occasionally until wilted and tender.
6) Season the Mediterranean Sautéed Kale with salt and black pepper to taste.
7) Serve hot as a delicious and nutritious side dish. Optionally, squeeze fresh lemon juice over the kale before serving for extra flavor.

NUTRITION

Cal 120; Fat 8 g; Carb 10 g;
Protein 4 g; Fiber: 3 g; Sodium: 250 mg

Green Bean Stew

| Prep time: 10 min | Cook time 25 min | Serving: 2 |

INGREDIENTS

- *1 pound green beans, trimmed and cut into bite-sized pieces*
- *2 tablespoons olive oil*
- *1 onion, finely chopped*
- *2 cloves garlic, minced*
- *1 (14.5-ounce) can diced tomatoes*
- *1 teaspoon dried oregano*
- *1 teaspoon dried thyme*
- *1/2 teaspoon paprika*
- *Salt and black pepper, to taste*
- *1/2 cup vegetable broth*
- *1 tablespoon tomato paste*
- *1/4 cup chopped fresh parsley for garnish*
- *Lemon wedges for serving (optional)*

1) In a large pot or Dutch oven, heat olive oil over medium heat. Add the chopped onion and cook for 3-4 minutes until softened.

2) Add minced garlic to the pot and cook for another 1-2 minutes until fragrant.

3) Stir in the diced tomatoes (with their juices), dried oregano, dried thyme, paprika, salt, and black pepper. Cook for 5 minutes, stirring occasionally.

4) Add the green beans to the pot and stir to coat them in the tomato mixture.

5) Pour in the vegetable broth and add the tomato paste. Stir well to combine.

6) Bring the stew to a simmer, then reduce the heat to low. Cover and let it simmer for 15-20 minutes or until the green beans are tender.

7) Taste and adjust seasoning if needed.

8) Serve the Mediterranean Green Bean Stew hot, garnished with chopped fresh parsley. Optionally, serve with lemon wedges on the side for squeezing over the stew.

NUTRITION

Cal 180; Fat 10 g; Carb 20 g; Protein 5 g; Fiber: 6 g; Sodium: 420 mg

Mediterranean Gnocchi

| Prep time: 15 min | Cook time 20 min | Serving: 2 |

INGREDIENTS

- *1 pound store-bought gnocchi*
- *2 tablespoons olive oil*
- *2 cloves garlic, minced*
- *1/2 cup sun-dried tomatoes, chopped*
- *1/4 cup Kalamata olives, pitted, and chopped*
- *2 cups baby spinach*
- *1 tablespoon capers, rinsed, and drained*
- *1/2 teaspoon dried oregano*
- *Salt and black pepper, to taste*
- *1/4 cup crumbled feta cheese, for garnish*
- *Fresh basil leaves, torn, for garnish*

1) Cook the gnocchi according to package instructions. Drain and set aside.
2) In a large skillet, heat olive oil over medium heat. Add minced gar-lic and cook for 1 minute until fragrant.
3) Add chopped sun-dried tomatoes, Kalamata olives, and capers to the skillet. Cook for 2-3 minutes until heated through.
4) Add the cooked gnocchi to the skillet along with baby spinach and dried oregano. Stir well to combine and cook for another 2-3 minutes until the spinach wilts.
5) Season the Mediterranean Gnocchi with salt and black pepper to taste.
6) Remove from heat and transfer to serving plates.
7) Garnish with crumbled feta cheese and torn fresh basil leaves.

NUTRITION

Cal 380; Fat 15 g; Carb 50 g; Protein 10 g; Fiber: 5 g; Sodium: 640 mg

Vegetarian Chili

Prep time: 15 min	Cook time 30 min	Serving: 2

INGREDIENTS

- *1 tablespoon olive oil*
- *1 onion, chopped*
- *3 cloves garlic, minced*
- *1 bell pepper, diced*
- *2 carrots, diced*
- *2 celery ribs, diced*
- *1 zucchini, diced*
- *1 (14.5-ounce) can diced tomatoes*
- *1 (15-ounce) can kidney beans, drained and rinsed*
- *1 (15-ounce) can black beans, drained and rinsed*
- *1 (15-ounce) can corn kernels, drained*
- *2 cups vegetable broth*
- *2 tablespoons chili powder*
- *1 teaspoon ground cumin*
- *1/2 teaspoon smoked paprika*
- *Salt and black pepper, to taste*
- *Fresh cilantro, chopped, for garnish*
- *Avocado slices, for serving (optional)*
- *Sour cream or Greek yogurt, for serving (optional)*
- *Shredded cheese for serving (optional)*
- *Lime wedges for serving (optional)*

1) In a large pot or Dutch oven, heat olive oil over medium heat. Add chopped onion and minced garlic, and sauté for 2-3 minutes until softened and fragrant.
2) Add diced bell pepper, carrots, celery, and zucchini to the pot. Cook for 5-7 minutes, stirring occasionally until the vegetables are tender.
3) Stir in diced tomatoes, kidney beans, black beans, corn kernels, vegetable broth, chili powder, ground cumin, and smoked paprika. Season with salt and black pepper to taste.
4) Bring the chili to a simmer, then reduce the heat to low. Cover and let it simmer for 20-25 minutes, stirring occasionally, to allow the flavors to meld together.
5) Taste and adjust seasoning if needed.
6) Serve the Vegetarian Chili hot, garnished with chopped fresh cilant-ro. Optionally, serve with avocado slices, sour cream or Greek yo-gurt, shredded cheese, and lime wedges on the side.

NUTRITION
Cal 280; Fat 5 g; Carb 50 g;
Protein 12 g; Fiber: 15 g; Sodium: 900 mg

Turkish Beet Greens

| Prep time: 10 min | Cook time 15 min | Serving: 4 |

INGREDIENTS

- *Greens from 1 bunch of beets, washed and chopped (about 4 cups)*
- *2 tablespoons olive oil*
- *1 onion, finely chopped*
- *3 cloves garlic, minced*
- *1 teaspoon ground cumin*
- *1/2 teaspoon ground coriander*
- *1/4 teaspoon red pepper flakes (adjust to taste)*
- *Salt and black pepper, to taste*
- *2 tablespoons lemon juice*
- *2 tablespoons chopped fresh parsley for garnish*
- *Lemon wedges for serving (optional)*

1) Heat olive oil in a large skillet over medium heat. Add chopped on-ion and cook for 3-4 minutes until softened.
2) Add minced garlic to the skillet and cook for another 1-2 minutes until fragrant.
3) Add the chopped beet greens to the skillet. Cook for 5-7 minutes, stirring occasionally until the greens are wilted and tender.
4) Stir in ground cumin, ground coriander, red pepper flakes, salt, and black pepper. Cook for another 1-2 minutes to allow the flavors to meld together.
5) Drizzle lemon juice over the cooked beet greens and stir well to combine.
6) Transfer the Turkish Beet Greens to a serving dish.
7) Garnish with chopped fresh parsley.
8) Serve hot as a delicious and nutritious side dish, with lemon wedges on the side for squeezing over the greens if desired.

NUTRITION
Cal 80; Fat 5 g; Carb 8 g;
Protein 3 g; Fiber: 3 g; Sodium: 320 mg

Zucchini and Tomato Casserole

Prep time: 15 min	Cook time 30 min	Serving: 2

INGREDIENTS

- *2 medium zucchini, sliced into rounds*
- *2 medium tomatoes, sliced into rounds*
- *1/2 onion, thinly sliced*
- *2 cloves garlic, minced*
- *2 tablespoons olive oil*
- *1/2 teaspoon dried oregano*
- *1/2 teaspoon dried basil*
- *Salt and black pepper, to taste*
- *1/4 cup grated Parmesan cheese*
- *Fresh basil leaves, chopped for garnish (optional)*

1) Preheat your oven to 375°F (190°C). Grease a small baking dish with olive oil or non-stick cooking spray.
2) In a skillet, heat 1 tablespoon of olive oil over medium heat. Add the sliced onion and minced garlic. Sauté for 2-3 minutes until softened and fragrant.
3) Arrange half of the sliced zucchini in the bottom of the prepared baking dish. Top with half of the sautéed onion and garlic mixture.
4) Layer half of the sliced tomatoes on top of the onions and garlic.
5) Drizzle the vegetables with the remaining tablespoon of olive oil. Sprinkle with dried oregano, dried basil, salt, and black pepper.
6) Repeat the layers with the remaining zucchini, onion mixture, and tomatoes.
7) Cover the baking dish with aluminum foil and bake in the preheated oven for 20 minutes.
8) Remove the foil and sprinkle the grated Parmesan cheese over the top of the casserole.
9) Return the casserole to the oven and bake, uncovered, for another 10 minutes or until the cheese is melted and bubbly.
10) Garnish with chopped fresh basil leaves, if desired, before serving.

NUTRITION
Cal 150; Fat 8 g; Carb 12 g;
Protein 6 g; Fiber: 4 g; Sodium: 350 mg

Roasted Brussels Sprouts and Pecans

| Prep time: 10 min | Cook time 20 min | Serving: 2 |

INGREDIENTS

- *1/2 pound Brussels sprouts, trimmed and halved*
- *2 tablespoons olive oil*
- *1/4 teaspoon salt*
- *1/4 teaspoon black pepper*
- *1/4 cup pecan halves*
- *1 tablespoon balsamic vinegar (optional)*

1) Preheat your oven to 400°F (200°C). Line a baking sheet with parchment paper.
2) In a bowl, toss the halved Brussels sprouts with olive oil, salt, and black pepper until evenly coated.
3) Spread the Brussels sprouts out on the prepared baking sheet in a single layer.
4) Roast in the preheated oven for 15 minutes.
5) After 15 minutes, remove the baking sheet from the oven and add the pecan halves. Toss them with the Brussels sprouts.
6) Return the baking sheet to the oven and roast for another 5 minutes or until the Brussels sprouts are tender and the pecans are toasted.
7) If desired, drizzle the roasted Brussels sprouts and pecans with bal-samic vinegar before serving.

NUTRITION
Cal 200; Fat 15 g; Carb 15 g; Protein 6 g; Fiber: 7 g; Sodium: 250 mg

Briami

Prep time: 15 min | Cook time: 45 min | Serving: 2

INGREDIENTS

- *1 medium eggplant, sliced into rounds*
- *1 medium zucchini, sliced into rounds*
- *1 medium potato, peeled, and sliced into rounds*
- *1 red bell pepper, sliced*
- *1 yellow bell pepper, sliced*
- *1 onion, thinly sliced*
- *2 cloves garlic, minced*
- *2 tomatoes, sliced*
- *2 tablespoons olive oil*
- *1 teaspoon dried oregano*
- *Salt and black pepper, to taste*
- *Fresh parsley, chopped for garnish (optional)*

1) Preheat your oven to 375°F (190°C). Grease a baking dish with olive oil or non-stick cooking spray.
2) Arrange the sliced eggplant, zucchini, potato, red bell pepper, yellow bell pepper, onion, garlic, and tomatoes in the prepared baking dish, alternating the vegetables and layering them evenly.
3) Drizzle olive oil over the vegetables. Sprinkle with dried oregano, salt, and black pepper.
4) Cover the baking dish with aluminum foil and bake in the preheated oven for 30 minutes.
5) After 30 minutes, remove the foil and continue baking for another 15 minutes or until the vegetables are tender and lightly browned.
6) Once cooked, remove from the oven and let it cool slightly.
7) Serve the Briami hot, garnished with chopped fresh parsley if desired.

NUTRITION

Cal 180; Fat 10 g; Carb 20 g; Protein 5 g; Fiber: 6 g; Sodium: 420 mg

Fasolakia

Prep time: 10 min | **Cook time:** 25 min | **Serving:** 2

INGREDIENTS

- *1/2 pound fresh green beans, trimmed and cut into bite-sized pieces*
- *1 tablespoon olive oil*
- *1 small onion, finely chopped*
- *2 cloves garlic, minced*
- *1 can (14.5 ounces) diced tomatoes*
- *1 teaspoon dried oregano*
- *Salt and black pepper, to taste*
- *1/4 cup chopped fresh parsley for garnish (optional)*
- *Crumbled feta cheese for serving (optional)*

1) Heat olive oil in a skillet over medium heat. Add chopped onion and cook until softened, about 3-4 minutes.
2) Add minced garlic to the skillet and cook for another 1 minute until fragrant.
3) Add the green beans to the skillet and sauté for 2-3 minutes, stirring occasionally.
4) Pour the diced tomatoes (with their juices) into the skillet. Add dried oregano, salt, and black pepper to taste. Stir to combine.
5) Bring the mixture to a simmer, then reduce the heat to low. Cover and let it cook for about 15-20 minutes or until the green beans are tender, stirring occasionally.
6) Once the green beans are cooked to your desired tenderness, remove the skillet from the heat.
7) Serve the Fasolakia hot, garnished with chopped fresh parsley and crumbled feta cheese if desired.

NUTRITION

Cal 120; Fat 7 g; Carb 14 g;
Protein 3 g; Fiber: 5 g; Sodium: 250 mg

Stuffed Eggplant with Onion and Tomato

Prep time: 15 min
Cook time: 40 min
Serving: 2

INGREDIENTS

- *1 large eggplant*
- *1 tablespoon olive oil*
- *1 small onion, finely chopped*
- *2 cloves garlic, minced*
- *1 medium tomato, diced*
- *1/4 cup breadcrumbs*
- *2 tablespoons grated Parmesan cheese*
- *1 tablespoon chopped fresh parsley*
- *Salt and black pepper, to taste*
- *Fresh basil leaves for garnish (optional)*

1) Preheat your oven to 375°F (190°C). Grease a baking dish with olive oil or non-stick cooking spray.

2) Cut the eggplant in half lengthwise. Score the flesh with a knife in a crisscross pattern, being careful not to pierce the skin. Scoop out the flesh from the center of each half, leaving about a 1/4-inch thick shell. Chop the scooped-out eggplant flesh and set aside.

3) Heat olive oil in a skillet over medium heat. Add chopped onion and minced garlic, and cook until softened, about 3-4 minutes.

4) Add the chopped eggplant flesh to the skillet and cook for another 5 minutes, stirring occasionally.

5) Stir in diced tomato, breadcrumbs, grated Parmesan cheese, chopped fresh parsley, salt, and black pepper. Cook for another 2-3 minutes until the mixture is heated through and well combined.

6) Spoon the filling mixture into the eggplant halves, pressing gently to pack it in.

7) Place the stuffed eggplant halves in the prepared baking dish. Cover the dish with aluminum foil.

8) Bake in the preheated oven for 25-30 minutes or until the eggplant is tender.

9) Remove the foil and bake for an additional 5-10 minutes or until the tops are golden brown.

10) Garnish with fresh basil leaves before serving, if desired.

NUTRITION
Cal 180; Fat 8 g; Carb 25 g;
Protein 4 g; Fiber: 9 g; Sodium: 320 mg

Stuffed Eggplant with Couscous and Pecans

| Prep time: 15 min | Cook time 40 min | Serving: 2 |

INGREDIENTS

- *1 large eggplant*
- *1/2 cup couscous*
- *1 cup vegetable broth*
- *1/4 cup chopped pecans*
- *1 tablespoon olive oil*
- *1 small onion, finely chopped*
- *2 cloves garlic, minced*
- *1/2 teaspoon ground cumin*
- *1/2 teaspoon paprika*
- *1/4 teaspoon cinnamon*
- *Salt and black pepper, to taste*
- *2 tablespoons chopped fresh parsley for garnish*

1) Preheat your oven to 375°F (190°C). Grease a baking dish with olive oil or non-stick cooking spray.

2) Cut the eggplant in half lengthwise. Score the flesh with a knife in a crisscross pattern, being careful not to pierce the skin. Scoop out the flesh from the center of each half, leaving about a 1/4-inch thick shell. Chop the scooped-out eggplant flesh and set aside.

3) In a small saucepan, bring the vegetable broth to a boil. Stir in the couscous, cover, and remove from heat. Let it sit for 5 minutes, then fluff with a fork.

4) In a skillet, heat olive oil over medium heat. Add chopped onion and minced garlic, and cook until softened, about 3-4 minutes.

5) Add the chopped eggplant flesh to the skillet and cook for another 5 minutes, stirring occasionally.

6) Stir in ground cumin, paprika, cinnamon, salt, and black pepper. Cook for another 1-2 minutes until fragrant.

7) In a large mixing bowl, combine the cooked couscous, sautéed eggplant mixture, and chopped pecans. Mix well to combine.

8) Spoon the couscous mixture into the eggplant halves, pressing gently to pack it in.

9) Place the stuffed eggplant halves in the prepared baking dish.
10) Bake in the preheated oven for 25-30 minutes or until the eggplant is tender.
11) Garnish with chopped fresh parsley before serving.

NUTRITION
Cal 320; Fat 12 g; Carb 47 g;
Protein 8 g; Fiber: 10 g; Sodium: 250 mg

SOUPS

Vegetable Soup

Prep time: 15 min	Cook time: 25 min		Serving: 2

INGREDIENTS

- *2 tablespoons olive oil*
- *2 cloves garlic, minced*
- *1 onion, diced*
- *1 zucchini, diced*
- *1 bell pepper, diced*
- *2 tomatoes, diced*
- *2 cups vegetable broth*
- *1 teaspoon dried oregano*
- *Salt and black pepper, to taste*
- *2 cups fresh spinach leaves*
- *Optional: 1 cup cooked beans (such as chickpeas or white beans)*

1) In a large pot, heat the olive oil over medium heat. Add the minced garlic and diced onion, and sauté for 2-3 minutes until softened.
2) Add the diced zucchini and bell pepper to the pot, and cook for another 3-4 minutes until they begin to soften.
3) Stir in the diced tomatoes, vegetable broth, dried oregano, salt, and black pepper. Bring the soup to a simmer.
4) Reduce the heat to low and let the soup simmer for 15-20 minutes, allowing the flavors to meld and the vegetables to become tender.
5) If using, add the cooked beans to the soup and let them heat through for a few minutes.
6) Stir in the fresh spinach leaves and cook for an additional 2-3 minutes until wilted.
7) Taste the soup and adjust seasoning if necessary.
8) Serve the Mediterranean Vegetable Soup hot, garnished with a driz-zle of olive oil and a sprinkle of freshly chopped parsley if desired.

NUTRITION

Cal 180; Fat 9 g; Carb 23 g; Protein 4 g; Fiber: 7 g; Sodium: 650 mg

Lentil and Spinach Soup

| Prep time: 10 min | Cook time: 30 min | Serving: 2 |

INGREDIENTS

- *1 tablespoon olive oil*
- *1 onion, diced*
- *2 cloves garlic, minced*
- *1 cup dried lentils, rinsed, and drained*
- *1 can (14 ounces) diced tomatoes*
- *4 cups vegetable broth*
- *2 cups fresh spinach leaves, chopped*
- *1 teaspoon ground cumin*
- *1 teaspoon ground coriander*
- *Pinch of red pepper flakes (optional)*
- *Salt and black pepper, to taste*

1) In a large pot, heat olive oil over medium heat. Add diced onion and minced garlic, and sauté until softened, about 3-4 minutes.

2) Add rinsed and drained lentils to the pot, along with diced tomatoes and vegetable broth. Stir to combine.

3) Bring the soup to a boil, then reduce the heat to low, cover, and simmer for 20-25 minutes or until the lentils are tender.

4) Stir in chopped spinach leaves, ground cumin, ground coriander, and a pinch of red pepper flakes (if using). Cook for an additional 5 minutes until the spinach is wilted and the flavors are well combined.

5) Season the soup with salt and black pepper to taste.

6) Serve the Lentil and Spinach Soup hot, garnished with a sprinkle of freshly chopped parsley or a drizzle of olive oil if desired.

NUTRITION

Cal 320; Fat 9 g; Carb 50 g;
Protein 18 g; Fiber: 18 g; Sodium: 1250 mg

Greek Lemon Chicken Soup (Avgolemono)

| Prep time: 10 min | Cook time 20 min | Serving: 2 |

INGREDIENTS

- *4 cups chicken broth*
- *1 cup shredded cooked chicken breast*
- *1/4 cup orzo pasta (substitute whole wheat or quinoa for lower carbs)*
- *2 large eggs*
- *Juice of 1 lemon (about 3-4 tablespoons)*
- *Salt and black pepper, to taste*
- *Fresh dill or parsley, chopped for garnish*

1) In a large pot, bring the chicken broth to a simmer over medium heat.

2) Add the shredded cooked chicken and orzo pasta to the pot. Cook for 8-10 minutes or until the orzo is tender.

3) In a mixing bowl, whisk together the eggs and lemon juice until well combined.

4) Once the orzo is cooked, ladle about 1 cup of the hot broth from the pot into the bowl with the egg-lemon mixture, whisking constantly to temper the eggs.

5) Gradually pour the egg-lemon mixture back into the pot with the soup, stirring continuously.

6) Cook the soup for another 2-3 minutes, stirring occasionally until it thickens slightly and the eggs are fully cooked.

7) Season the soup with salt and black pepper to taste.

8) Serve the Greek Lemon Chicken Soup hot, garnished with chopped fresh dill or parsley.

NUTRITION

Cal 300; Fat 9 g; Carb 25 g; Protein 25 g; Fiber: 4 g; Sodium: 900 mg

Tuscan White Bean Soup

| Prep time: 10 min | Cook time 25 min | Serving: 2 |

INGREDIENTS

- *1 tablespoon olive oil*
- *1 onion, diced*
- *2 cloves garlic, minced*
- *1 can (15 ounces) white beans, drained and rinsed*
- *1 can (14.5 ounces) diced tomatoes*
- *2 cups vegetable broth*
- *2 cups chopped kale leaves*
- *1 teaspoon dried rosemary*
- *1 teaspoon dried thyme*
- *Salt and black pepper, to taste*
- *Extra olive oil for drizzling (optional)*

1) In a large pot, heat olive oil over medium heat. Add diced onion and minced garlic, and sauté until softened, about 3-4 minutes.

2) Add drained and rinsed white beans, diced tomatoes, vegetable broth, chopped kale leaves, dried rosemary, and dried thyme to the pot. Stir to combine.

3) Bring the soup to a simmer, then reduce the heat to low. Cover and let it simmer for 15-20 minutes, allowing the flavors to meld and the kale to wilt.

4) Season the soup with salt and black pepper to taste.

5) Once the soup is ready, ladle it into bowls and drizzle each serving with a bit of extra olive oil, if desired.

NUTRITION

Cal 280; Fat 6 g; Carb 48 g;
Protein 13 g; Fiber: 13 g; Sodium: 940 mg

Chunky Mediterranean Tomato Soup

Prep time: 10 min	Cook time 25 min	Serving: 2

INGREDIENTS

- *1 tablespoon olive oil*
- *1/2 onion, chopped*
- *2 cloves garlic, minced*
- *1 carrot, diced*
- *1 celery stalk, diced*
- *1/2 teaspoon dried oregano*
- *1/2 teaspoon dried basil*
- *1/4 teaspoon red pepper flakes (adjust to taste)*
- *1 can (14.5 ounces) diced tomatoes*
- *1 cup vegetable broth*
- *Salt and black pepper, to taste*
- *Fresh basil leaves, chopped for garnish (optional)*
- *Croutons, for serving (optional)*

1) Heat olive oil in a pot over medium heat. Add chopped onion and cook until softened, about 3-4 minutes.
2) Add minced garlic to the pot and cook for another 1 minute until fragrant.
3) Add diced carrot and celery to the pot. Cook for 5 minutes, stirring occasionally until the vegetables are slightly softened.
4) Stir in dried oregano, dried basil, and red pepper flakes. Cook for another 1 minute to toast the spices.
5) Pour in the diced tomatoes (with their juices) and vegetable broth. Bring the mixture to a simmer.
6) Reduce the heat to low and let the soup simmer, uncovered, for 15 minutes to allow the flavors to meld together.
7) Season the soup with salt and black pepper to taste.
8) Ladle the Chunky Mediterranean Tomato Soup into bowls. Garnish with chopped fresh basil leaves if desired.
9) Serve hot, optionally with croutons on top for added texture.

NUTRITION

Cal 180; Fat 8 g; Carb 24 g
Protein 4 g; Fiber: 5 g; Sodium: 780 mg

Chicken, Chickpea & Zucchini Soup

| Prep time: 10 min | Cook time 25 min | Serving: 2 |

INGREDIENTS

- *1 tablespoon olive oil*
- *1/2 onion, finely chopped*
- *2 cloves garlic, minced*
- *1 small zucchini, diced*
- *1 boneless, skinless chicken breast, diced*
- *1 can (14.5 ounces) diced tomatoes*
- *1 can (14.5 ounces) chickpeas, drained, and rinsed*
- *2 cups chicken broth*
- *1 teaspoon dried oregano*
- *1/2 teaspoon dried thyme*
- *Salt and black pepper, to taste*
- *Fresh parsley, chopped for garnish (optional)*
- *Crusty bread for serving (optional)*

1) Heat olive oil in a pot over medium heat. Add chopped onion and cook until softened, about 3-4 minutes.
2) Add minced garlic to the pot and cook for another 1 minute until fragrant.
3) Add diced zucchini to the pot and cook for 2-3 minutes until slightly softened.
4) Add diced chicken breast to the pot and cook until lightly browned on all sides, about 5-7 minutes.
5) Pour in the diced tomatoes (with their juices), drained and rinsed chickpeas, and chicken broth. Stir to combine.
6) Season the soup with dried oregano, dried thyme, salt, and black pepper to taste.
7) Bring the soup to a simmer. Reduce the heat to low, cover, and let it simmer for 15 minutes to allow the flavors to meld together.
8) Taste and adjust seasoning if needed.
9) Ladle the Mediterranean Chicken, Chickpea & Zucchini Soup into bowls. Garnish with chopped fresh parsley if desired.
10) Serve hot, optionally with crusty bread on the side for dipping.

NUTRITION
Cal 300; Fat 12 g; Carb 22 g;
Protein 24 g; Fiber: 6 g; Sodium: 600 mg

Chicken & Kale Soup

| Prep time: 10 min | Cook time 25 min | Serving: 2 |

INGREDIENTS

- *1 tablespoon olive oil*
- *1/2 onion, finely chopped*
- *2 cloves garlic, minced*
- *1 boneless, skinless chicken breast, diced*
- *4 cups chicken broth*
- *2 cups kale, chopped*
- *1 carrot, diced*
- *1 celery stalk, diced*
- *1/2 teaspoon dried thyme*
- *Salt and black pepper, to taste*
- *Fresh parsley, chopped for garnish (optional)*
- *Lemon wedges for serving (optional)*

1) Heat olive oil in a pot over medium heat. Add chopped onion and cook until softened, about 3-4 minutes.
2) Add minced garlic to the pot and cook for another 1 minute until fragrant.
3) Add diced chicken breast to the pot and cook until lightly browned on all sides, about 5-7 minutes.
4) Pour in the chicken broth and bring to a simmer.
5) Add chopped kale, diced carrot, diced celery, and dried thyme to the pot. Stir to combine.
6) Season the soup with salt and black pepper to taste.
7) Cover and let the soup simmer for 15 minutes or until the vegetables are tender and the chicken is cooked through.
8) Taste and adjust seasoning if needed.
9) Ladle the Chicken & Kale Soup into bowls. Garnish with chopped fresh parsley if desired.
10) Serve hot, optionally with lemon wedges on the side for squeezing over the soup.

NUTRITION

Cal 250; Fat 8 g; Carb 14 g; Protein 30 g; Fiber: 3 g; Sodium: 700 mg

Chicken & Bok Choy Soup with Ginger & Mushrooms

| Prep time: 10 min | Cook time 25 min | Serving: 2 |

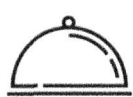

INGREDIENTS

- *1 tablespoon olive oil*
- *2 cloves garlic, minced*
- *1 teaspoon fresh ginger, minced*
- *1 boneless, skinless chicken breast, thinly sliced*
- *4 cups chicken broth*
- *1 cup mushrooms, sliced*
- *2 baby bok choy, chopped*
- *2 green onions, chopped*
- *1 tablespoon soy sauce*
- *Salt and black pepper, to taste*
- *Sesame seeds for garnish (optional)*

1) Heat olive oil in a pot over medium heat. Add minced garlic and ginger, and cook for 1-2 minutes until fragrant.
2) Add thinly sliced chicken breast to the pot and cook until lightly browned on all sides, about 5 minutes.
3) Pour in the chicken broth and bring to a simmer.
4) Add sliced mushrooms to the pot and let it simmer for 5 minutes.
5) Add chopped baby bok choy and chopped green onions to the pot. Stir to combine.
6) Season the soup with soy sauce, salt, and black pepper to taste.
7) Cover and let the soup simmer for another 10 minutes or until the chicken is cooked through and the vegetables are tender.
8) Taste and adjust seasoning if needed.
9) Ladle the Chicken & Bok Choy Soup into bowls. Garnish with sesame seeds if desired.

NUTRITION

Cal 220; Fat 8 g; Carb 10 g;
Protein 28 g; Fiber: 4 g; Sodium: 800 mg

Rainbow Minestrone

Prep time: 10 min | Cook time: 20 min | Serving: 2

INGREDIENTS

- *1 tablespoon olive oil*
- *1/2 onion, diced*
- *1 carrot, diced*
- *1 celery stalk, diced*
- *2 cloves garlic, minced*
- *1 small zucchini, diced*
- *1 small yellow squash, diced*
- *1/2 cup diced tomatoes (canned or fresh)*
- *2 cups vegetable broth*
- *1/2 cup small pasta (such as ditalini or small shells)*
- *1/2 teaspoon dried thyme*
- *1/2 teaspoon dried oregano*
- *Salt and black pepper, to taste*
- *1 cup fresh spinach leaves*
- *Grated Parmesan cheese for serving (optional)*
- *Fresh basil leaves, chopped for garnish (optional)*

1) Heat olive oil in a pot over medium heat. Add diced onion, carrot, and celery. Cook for 5 minutes or until vegetables are softened.
2) Add minced garlic and cook for another minute until fragrant.
3) Add diced zucchini and yellow squash to the pot. Cook for 2-3 minutes.
4) Stir in diced tomatoes, vegetable broth, dried thyme, dried oregano, salt, and black pepper. Bring to a simmer.
5) Add small pasta to the pot and cook according to package instructions, usually about 8-10 minutes.
6) Once pasta is cooked, add fresh spinach leaves to the pot and cook for 1-2 minutes until wilted.
7) Taste and adjust seasoning if necessary.
8) Ladle the Rainbow Minestrone into bowls. If desired, sprinkle with grated Parmesan cheese and garnish with chopped fresh basil leaves.

NUTRITION

Cal 260; Fat 5 g; Carb 45 g;
Protein 10 g; Fiber: 10 g; Sodium: 800 mg

Bean & Barley Soup

| Prep time: 10 min | Cook time 45 min | Serving: 2 |

INGREDIENTS

- *1 tablespoon olive oil*
- *1 onion, diced*
- *2 cloves garlic, minced*
- *2 carrots, diced*
- *2 celery stalks, diced*
- *1 cup dried beans (such as navy beans or cannellini beans), soaked overnight and drained*
- *1/2 cup pearl barley*
- *6 cups vegetable broth*
- *1 bay leaf*
- *1 teaspoon dried thyme*
- *Salt and pepper, to taste*
- *Chopped fresh parsley for garnish (optional)*
- *Grated Parmesan cheese for serving (optional)*

1) In a large pot, heat the olive oil over medium heat. Add the diced onion and cook until softened, about 5 minutes.

2) Add the minced garlic and cook for another minute until fragrant.

3) Add the diced carrots and celery to the pot and cook for 5 minutes until slightly softened.

4) Add the soaked and drained beans, pearl barley, vegetable broth, bay leaf, and dried thyme to the pot. Stir to combine.

5) Bring the soup to a boil, then reduce the heat to low and simmer, partially covered, for about 35-40 minutes or until the beans and barley are tender.

6) Season the soup with salt and pepper to taste.

7) Remove the bay leaf from the soup before serving.

8) Ladle the Bean & Barley Soup into bowls. If desired, garnish with chopped fresh parsley and serve with grated Parmesan cheese on the side.

NUTRITION

Cal 280; Fat 2 g; Carb 52 g;
Protein 15 g; Fiber: 14 g; Sodium: 500 mg

RICE, GRAIN, PASTA, COUSCOUS

Mediterranean Kale Fried Rice

| Prep time: 10 min | Cook time 15 min | Serving: 2 |

INGREDIENTS

- *1 cup cooked brown rice*
- *2 tablespoons olive oil*
- *2 cloves garlic, minced*
- *1/2 onion, finely chopped*
- *2 cups kale, stems removed, and leaves chopped*
- *1 medium tomato, diced*
- *1/4 cup Kalamata olives, pitted, and chopped*
- *2 tablespoons crumbled feta cheese*
- *1 tablespoon lemon juice*
- *Salt and pepper, to taste*
- *Fresh parsley, chopped for garnish (optional)*

1) Heat olive oil in a large skillet or wok over medium heat. Add minced garlic and chopped onion. Cook until softened, about 3-4 minutes.

2) Add chopped kale to the skillet. Cook until wilted, about 2-3 minutes.

3) Add cooked brown rice to the skillet. Stir well to combine with the kale mixture.

4) Add diced tomato and Kalamata olives to the skillet. Cook for another 2-3 minutes, stirring occasionally.

5) Drizzle lemon juice over the rice mixture. Season with salt and pepper to taste. Stir to combine.

6) Cook for an additional 2-3 minutes or until the rice is heated through and the flavors are well combined.

7) Remove the skillet from heat. Sprinkle crumbled feta cheese over the rice mixture.

8) Serve the Mediterranean Kale Fried Rice hot, garnished with chopped fresh parsley if desired.

NUTRITION

Cal 280; Fat 10 g; Carb 40 g;
Protein 10 g; Fiber: 5 g; Sodium: 580 mg

Mediterranean Tomato Rice

Prep time: 10 min | Cook time: 20 min | Serving: 2

INGREDIENTS

- 2 garlic cloves, minced
- 1/2 cup onions, chopped
- 1 tablespoon olive oil
- 1/2 teaspoon dried thyme
- 1/2 cup green bell pepper, diced
- 1/2 tablespoon tomato paste
- 1 1/2 cups cooked rice
- 1/2 cup celery, thinly sliced
- 1/4 teaspoon dried marjoram
- 1/2 can (about 7.5 ounces) tomatoes, drained, and liquid reserved
- Salt and black pepper, to taste

1) In a skillet, heat olive oil over medium heat. Add minced garlic and chopped onions. Cook until onions are translucent, about 3-4 minutes.
2) Add dried thyme and diced green bell pepper to the skillet. Cook for another 2-3 minutes until peppers are slightly softened.
3) Stir in tomato paste and cook for 1 minute, stirring constantly.
4) Add cooked rice and thinly sliced celery to the skillet. Mix well to combine.
5) Sprinkle dried marjoram over the rice mixture. Pour in the drained tomatoes, breaking them up with a spoon as you add them. Reserve some of the liquid from the canned tomatoes.
6) Season with salt and black pepper to taste. If the mixture seems dry, add a little of the reserved tomato liquid.
7) Cook for another 5-7 minutes, stirring occasionally until the flavors are well combined and the rice is heated through.
8) Adjust seasoning if necessary.

NUTRITION

Cal 420; Fat 14 g; Carb 67 g; Protein 7 g; Fiber: 5 g; Sodium: 320 mg

Mediterranean Pasta Salad

Prep time: 15 min	Cook time 10 min	Serving: 2

INGREDIENTS

- *6 ounces pasta (such as penne or fusilli)*
- *1/2 cucumber, diced*
- *1 cup cherry tomatoes, halved*
- *1/4 cup red onion, thinly sliced*
- *1/4 cup Kalamata olives, pitted, and sliced*
- *1/4 cup marinated artichoke hearts, chopped*
- *1/4 cup crumbled feta cheese*
- *1/2 cup cooked chickpeas (optional, for extra protein)*
- **For the lemon-herb vinaigrette:**
- *2 tablespoons olive oil*
- *1 tablespoon lemon juice*
- *1 teaspoon Dijon mustard*
- *1 clove garlic, minced*
- *1 teaspoon dried oregano*
- *1/2 teaspoon dried basil*
- *Salt and black pepper, to taste*

1) Cook the pasta according to the package instructions until al dente. Drain and rinse under cold water to stop the cooking process.

2) In a large mixing bowl, combine the cooked pasta with diced cucumber, halved cherry tomatoes, thinly sliced red onion, sliced Kalamata olives, chopped marinated artichoke hearts, crumbled feta cheese, and cooked chickpeas (if using).

3) In a small bowl, whisk together olive oil, lemon juice, Dijon mustard, minced garlic, dried oregano, dried basil, salt, and black pepper to make the lemon-herb vinaigrette.

4) Pour the lemon-herb vinaigrette over the pasta salad ingredients in the mixing bowl.

5) Toss the pasta salad gently until all ingredients are evenly coated with the vinaigrette.

6) Taste and adjust seasoning if needed.

7) Once the pasta salad is well mixed, transfer it to serving plates or bowls.

8) Serve the Mediterranean Pasta Salad immediately, or refrigerate for 30 minutes to allow the flavors to meld before serving.

NUTRITION
Cal 450; Fat 18 g; Carb 60 g;
Protein 14 g; Fiber: 8 g; Sodium: 400 mg

Brown Rice Pilaf

Prep time: 10 min | Cook time: 40 min | Serving: 2

INGREDIENTS

- *1 cup brown rice*
- *2 cups water or vegetable broth*
- *1 carrot, diced*
- *1 bell pepper, diced*
- *1/2 onion, diced*
- *2 cloves garlic, minced*
- *Zest of 1 lemon*
- *1/4 cup pine nuts, toasted*
- *2 tablespoons olive oil*
- *Salt and black pepper, to taste*
- *Fresh parsley, chopped for garnish (optional)*

1) Rinse the brown rice under cold water until the water runs clear.

2) In a medium saucepan, combine the rinsed brown rice with water or vegetable broth. Bring to a boil over high heat.

3) Once boiling, reduce the heat to low, cover, and simmer for 35-40 minutes or until the rice is tender and the liquid is absorbed.

4) While the rice is cooking, heat olive oil in a skillet over medium heat.

5) Add minced garlic to the skillet and sauté for about 1 minute until fragrant.

6) Add diced carrot, bell pepper, and onion to the skillet. Cook, stirring occasionally, for about 5-7 minutes until the vegetables are tender.

7) Once the rice is cooked, fluff it with a fork and transfer it to a large mixing bowl.

8) Add the cooked vegetables, lemon zest, and toasted pine nuts to the bowl with the rice.

9) Season the pilaf with salt and black pepper to taste, and toss gently to combine all ingredients.

10) Garnish the Mediterranean Brown Rice Pilaf with chopped fresh parsley if desired.

11) Serve the pilaf hot as a side dish or as a main course.

NUTRITION
Cal 380; Fat 15 g; Carb 54 g;
Protein 8 g; Fiber: 6 g; Sodium: 10 mg

Mediterranean Style Spaghetti Squash

| Prep time: 10 min | Cook time 45 min | Serving: 2 |

INGREDIENTS

- *1 medium spaghetti squash*
- *1 cup diced tomatoes*
- *1/4 cup black olives, sliced*
- *2 tablespoons capers*
- *3 cloves garlic, minced*
- *2 tablespoons olive oil*
- *Fresh herbs (such as basil, parsley, or oregano), chopped*
- *Salt and black pepper, to taste*
- *Grated Parmesan cheese for serving (optional)*

1) Preheat your oven to 400°F (200°C).
2) Cut the spaghetti squash in half lengthwise and scoop out the seeds.
3) Drizzle the cut sides of the squash with olive oil and season with salt and black pepper.
4) Place the squash halves cut side down on a baking sheet lined with parchment paper or aluminum foil.
5) Roast in the preheated oven for 40-45 minutes or until the squash is tender and easily pierced with a fork.
6) While the squash is roasting, prepare the Mediterranean-style topping. In a mixing bowl, combine diced tomatoes, sliced black olives, capers, minced garlic, chopped fresh herbs, and olive oil. Season with salt and black pepper to taste.
7) Once the spaghetti squash is cooked, remove it from the oven and let it cool slightly.
8) Use a fork to scrape the flesh of the squash into strands.
9) Transfer the spaghetti squash strands to a large mixing bowl and add the Mediterranean-style topping. Toss gently to combine all ingredients.
10) Serve the Mediterranean Style Spaghetti Squash hot, garnished with grated Parmesan cheese if desired.

NUTRITION
Cal 220; Fat 14 g; Carb 22 g;
Protein 3 g; Fiber: 6 g; Sodium: 560 mg

Pasta Primavera

Prep time: 15 min | Cook time: 15 min | Serving: 2

INGREDIENTS

- *6 ounces whole wheat pasta*
- *1 bell pepper, thinly sliced*
- *1 zucchini, thinly sliced*
- *1 cup cherry tomatoes, halved*
- *1 cup broccoli florets*
- *3 cloves garlic, minced*
- *2 tablespoons olive oil*
- *1 teaspoon dried Italian herbs (such as basil, oregano, thyme)*
- *Salt and black pepper, to taste*
- *Grated Parmesan cheese for serving (optional)*
- *Fresh basil leaves, chopped for garnish (optional)*

1) Cook the whole wheat pasta according to the package instructions until al dente. Drain and set aside.
2) In a large skillet or pan, heat olive oil over medium heat.
3) Add minced garlic to the skillet and sauté for about 1 minute until fragrant.
4) Add thinly sliced bell pepper, zucchini, cherry tomatoes, and broccoli florets to the skillet. Cook, stirring occasionally, for about 5-7 minutes until the vegetables are tender-crisp.
5) Sprinkle dried Italian herbs over the sautéed vegetables. Season with salt and black pepper to taste. Stir well to combine.
6) Add the cooked whole wheat pasta to the skillet with the sautéed vegetables.
7) Toss the pasta and vegetables together until evenly combined.
8) Once the pasta primavera is heated through, remove the skillet from heat.
9) Serve the Pasta Primavera with Whole Wheat Pasta hot, garnished with grated Parmesan cheese and chopped fresh basil leaves if desired.

NUTRITION
Cal 350; Fat 11 g; Carb 54 g;
Protein 12 g; Fiber: 10 g; Sodium: 110 mg

Lemon Garlic Chickpea Pasta

Prep time: 10 min	Cook time 15 min	Serving: 2

INGREDIENTS

- *6 ounces whole wheat or chickpea pasta*
- *1 can (14 ounces) chickpeas, drained, and rinsed*
- *3 cloves garlic, minced*
- *2 tablespoons olive oil*
- *2 tablespoons lemon juice*
- *Zest of 1 lemon*
- *Salt and black pepper, to taste*
- *Chopped parsley for garnish*

1) Cook the whole wheat or chickpea pasta according to the package instructions until al dente. Drain and set aside.
2) In a large skillet or pan, heat olive oil over medium heat.
3) Add minced garlic to the skillet and sauté for about 1 minute until fragrant.
4) Add the drained and rinsed chickpeas to the skillet. Cook, stirring occasionally, for about 5-7 minutes until the chickpeas are slightly crispy.
5) Once the chickpeas are cooked, add cooked pasta to the skillet.
6) Pour lemon juice over the pasta and chickpeas. Add lemon zest as well.
7) Season with salt and black pepper to taste. Toss everything together until the pasta is well coated with the lemon garlic sauce.
8) Once the pasta is heated through and well mixed with the chickpeas and sauce, remove the skillet from heat.
9) Serve the Lemon Garlic Chickpea Pasta hot, garnished with chopped parsley for freshness.

NUTRITION
Cal 390; Fat 12 g; Carb 58 g;
Protein 14 g; Fiber: 12 g; Sodium: 300 mg

Fakorizo

| Prep time: 10 min | Cook time 30 min | Serving: 2 |

INGREDIENTS

- *1/2 cup dried brown lentils, rinsed*
- *1/2 cup long-grain white rice*
- *2 cups vegetable broth*
- *2 tablespoons olive oil*
- *1 small onion, finely chopped*
- *2 cloves garlic, minced*
- *1 carrot, diced*
- *1 celery stalk, diced*
- *1/2 teaspoon dried oregano*
- *1/2 teaspoon dried thyme*
- *Salt and black pepper, to taste*
- *Lemon wedges for serving (optional)*
- *Chopped fresh parsley for garnish (optional)*

1) In a medium-sized pot, combine the vegetable broth and rinsed brown lentils. Bring to a boil over medium-high heat, then reduce the heat to low and let simmer for 15 minutes.
2) Add the rice to the pot with the lentils. Cover and continue to simmer for another 15 minutes or until the rice and lentils are tender and most of the liquid has been absorbed.
3) In a separate skillet, heat the olive oil over medium heat. Add the chopped onion and cook until translucent, about 3-4 minutes.
4) Add the minced garlic to the skillet and cook for an additional minute until fragrant.
5) Stir in the diced carrot and celery, and cook for 5-7 minutes until the vegetables are softened.
6) Add the cooked lentils and rice to the skillet with the vegetables. Mix well to combine.
7) Season with dried oregano, dried thyme, salt, and black pepper to taste. Stir until the herbs are evenly distributed.
8) Cook for an additional 2-3 minutes, allowing the flavors to meld together.
9) Serve the Fakorizo hot, optionally with lemon wedges on the side for squeezing over the dish and garnished with chopped fresh parsley.

NUTRITION

Cal 320; Fat 10 g; Carb 45 g;
Protein 15 g; Fiber: 8 g; Sodium: 580 mg

Spanakorizo

| Prep time: 10 min | Cook time 25 min | Serving: 2 |

INGREDIENTS

- *1 cup long-grain white rice*
- *2 tablespoons olive oil*
- *1 small onion, finely chopped*
- *2 cloves garlic, minced*
- *1 pound fresh spinach, washed, and roughly chopped*
- *1/2 teaspoon dried dill*
- *1/2 teaspoon dried oregano*
- *Salt and black pepper, to taste*
- *Juice of 1 lemon*
- *Lemon wedges for serving (optional)*
- *Crumbled feta cheese for serving (optional)*

1) Rinse the rice under cold water until the water runs clear. Drain and set aside.
2) In a large skillet or pot, heat the olive oil over medium heat. Add the chopped onion and cook until translucent, about 3-4 minutes.
3) Add the minced garlic to the skillet and cook for another minute until fragrant.
4) Add the chopped spinach to the skillet in batches, allowing each batch to wilt before adding more. Cook until all the spinach is wilted, about 5 minutes.
5) Stir in the dried dill and dried oregano, and season with salt and black pepper to taste.
6) Add the rinsed rice to the skillet and stir to combine with the spinach mixture.
7) Pour enough water into the skillet to cover the rice and spinach by about 1 inch. Bring to a boil, then reduce the heat to low, cover, and simmer for 15-20 minutes or until the rice is tender and the liquid is absorbed.
8) Once the rice is cooked, remove the skillet from heat and squeeze the juice of 1 lemon over the Spanakorizo. Stir to combine.
9) Serve the Spanakorizo hot, optionally with lemon wedges on the side for squeezing over the dish and crumbled feta cheese on top.

NUTRITION
Cal 280; Fat 8 g; Carb 45 g;
Protein 10 g; Fiber: 5 g; Sodium: 580 mg

Rotini with Spinach, Cherry Tomatoes, and Feta

| Prep time: 10 min | Cook time 15 min | Serving: 2 |

INGREDIENTS

- *6 ounces rotini pasta*
- *2 tablespoons olive oil*
- *2 cloves garlic, minced*
- *2 cups baby spinach leaves*
- *1 cup cherry tomatoes, halved*
- *2 tablespoons balsamic vinegar*
- *Salt and black pepper, to taste*
- *1/4 cup crumbled feta cheese*
- *Fresh basil leaves, chopped for garnish (optional)*

1) Cook the rotini pasta according to package instructions until al dente. Drain and set aside.
2) In a large skillet, heat the olive oil over medium heat. Add the minced garlic and cook for 1 minute until fragrant.
3) Add the baby spinach leaves to the skillet and cook until wilted, about 2-3 minutes.
4) Stir in the cherry tomatoes and cook for another 2-3 minutes until they start to soften.
5) Add the cooked rotini pasta to the skillet. Drizzle with balsamic vinegar and toss everything together until well combined.
6) Season with salt and black pepper to taste.
7) Remove the skillet from heat and sprinkle crumbled feta cheese over the pasta mixture.
8) Serve the Rotini with Spinach, Cherry Tomatoes, and Feta hot, garnished with chopped fresh basil leaves if desired.

NUTRITION

Cal 380; Fat 12 g; Carb 55 g; Protein 14 g; Fiber: 5 g; Sodium: 480 mg

Puglia-Style Pasta with Broccoli Sauce

| Prep time: 10 min | Cook time 20 min | Serving: 2 |

INGREDIENTS

- *6 ounces pasta (such as penne or orecchiette)*
- *2 tablespoons olive oil*
- *2 cloves garlic, minced*
- *1 small head of broccoli, florets separated (about 2 cups)*
- *1/4 cup vegetable broth*
- *Zest of 1 lemon*
- *Salt and black pepper, to taste*
- *Grated Parmesan cheese for serving (optional)*
- *Red pepper flakes for serving (optional)*

1) Cook the pasta according to package instructions until al dente. Drain and set aside, reserving 1/2 cup of pasta water.

2) In a large skillet, heat the olive oil over medium heat. Add the minced garlic and cook for 1 minute until fragrant.

3) Add the broccoli florets to the skillet and sauté for 3-4 minutes until they start to soften.

4) Pour in the vegetable broth and cover the skillet. Let the broccoli steam for another 3-4 minutes until tender.

5) Use a potato masher or fork to mash the broccoli into a rough sauce consistency. If needed, add some of the reserved pasta water to reach your desired sauce consistency.

6) Stir in the lemon zest and season the broccoli sauce with salt and black pepper to taste.

7) Add the cooked pasta to the skillet with the broccoli sauce. Toss everything together until well combined and heated through.

8) Serve the Puglia-Style Pasta with Broccoli Sauce hot, optionally topped with grated Parmesan cheese and red pepper flakes for extra flavor.

NUTRITION

Cal 350; Fat 12 g; Carb 45 g; Protein 14 g; Fiber: 5 g; Sodium: 430 mg

Orzo with Feta and Marinated Peppers

Prep time: 10 min | Cook time: 15 min | Serving: 2

INGREDIENTS

- *1 cup orzo pasta*
- *2 tablespoons olive oil*
- *2 cloves garlic, minced*
- *1/2 cup marinated peppers, diced (from a jar or homemade)*
- *1/4 cup crumbled feta cheese*
- *2 tablespoons chopped fresh parsley*
- *Salt and black pepper, to taste*
- *Lemon wedges for serving (optional)*

1) Cook the orzo pasta according to package instructions until al dente. Drain and set aside.
2) In a large skillet, heat the olive oil over medium heat. Add the minced garlic and sauté for 1 minute until fragrant.
3) Add the diced marinated peppers to the skillet and cook for 2-3 minutes, stirring occasionally.
4) Add the cooked orzo pasta to the skillet with the peppers. Toss everything together until well combined.
5) Stir in the crumbled feta cheese and chopped fresh parsley. Season with salt and black pepper to taste.
6) Cook for another 2-3 minutes, stirring occasionally until the feta cheese starts to melt and everything is heated through.
7) Serve the Orzo with Feta and Marinated Peppers hot, optionally with lemon wedges on the side for squeezing over the dish.

NUTRITION

Cal 380; Fat 12 g; Carb 55 g; Protein 14 g; Fiber: 3 g; Sodium: 580 mg

Mediterranean Grain Tabbouleh

| Prep time: 15 min | Cook time 20 min | Serving: 4 |

INGREDIENTS

- *1 cup bulgur wheat*
- *2 cups water or vegetable broth*
- *2 cups cherry tomatoes, halved*
- *1 cucumber, diced*
- *1/2 cup fresh parsley, chopped*
- *1/4 cup fresh mint leaves, chopped*
- *1/4 cup red onion, finely chopped*
- *1/4 cup Kalamata olives, pitted, and chopped*
- *1/4 cup crumbled feta cheese*
- *2 tablespoons extra-virgin olive oil*
- *2 tablespoons lemon juice*
- *1 clove garlic, minced*
- *Salt and pepper, to taste*

1) In a medium saucepan, bring the water or vegetable broth to a boil. Stir in the bulgur wheat, cover, and reduce heat to low. Simmer for 15-20 minutes or until the bulgur is tender and the liquid is absorbed. Remove from heat and let it cool.

2) In a large mixing bowl, combine the cooked bulgur wheat, halved cherry tomatoes, diced cucumber, chopped fresh parsley, chopped fresh mint leaves, finely chopped red onion, and chopped Kalamata olives.

3) In a small bowl, whisk together the extra-virgin olive oil, lemon juice, minced garlic, salt, and pepper to make the dressing.

4) Pour the dressing over the bulgur wheat and vegetable mixture. Toss everything together until well combined.

5) Sprinkle crumbled feta cheese over the top and gently toss to incorporate.

6) Serve the Mediterranean Grain Tabbouleh chilled or at room temperature.

NUTRITION
Cal 320; Fat 10 g; Carb 50 g;
Protein 10 g; Fiber: 8 g; Sodium: 380 mg

Pesto Chicken Quinoa Bowls

Prep time: 15 min | Cook time: 25 min | Serving: 4

INGREDIENTS

- *For the chicken:*
- 4 boneless, skinless chicken breasts
- Salt and black pepper, to taste
- 2 tablespoons olive oil
- 1/4 cup pesto sauce
- *For the quinoa:*
- 1 cup quinoa, rinsed
- 2 cups chicken broth or water
- Salt, to taste
- *For the bowl:*
- 2 cups cherry tomatoes, halved
- 1 cucumber, diced
- 1/4 cup red onion, thinly sliced
- 1/4 cup Kalamata olives, pitted and halved
- 1/4 cup crumbled feta cheese
- 1/4 cup pine nuts, toasted (optional)
- Fresh basil leaves for garnish (optional)

1) Preheat the oven to 400°F (200°C). Season the chicken breasts with salt and black pepper on both sides.

2) Heat olive oil in an oven-safe skillet over medium-high heat. Add the chicken breasts and cook for 2-3 minutes on each side until golden brown.

3) Transfer the skillet to the preheated oven and bake for 15-20 minutes or until the chicken is cooked through (internal temperature of 165°F/75°C).

4) While the chicken is cooking, prepare the quinoa. In a medium saucepan, combine the quinoa and chicken broth or water. Bring to a boil, then reduce heat to low, cover, and simmer for 15 minutes or until the quinoa is cooked and the liquid is absorbed. Fluff with a fork and season with salt to taste.

5) In a large mixing bowl, combine the halved cherry tomatoes, diced cucumber, thinly sliced red onion, halved Kalamata olives, and crumbled feta cheese.

6) Once the chicken is cooked, remove it from the oven and let it rest for a few minutes before slicing it into strips.

7) To assemble the bowls, divide the cooked quinoa among serving bowls. Top with the mixed vegetables and crumbled feta cheese. Arrange the sliced chicken on top.

8) Drizzle pesto sauce over the chicken and sprinkle toasted pine nuts on top, if using. Garnish with fresh basil leaves, if desired.

NUTRITION

Cal 450; Fat 20 g; Carb 35 g;
Protein 30 g; Fiber: 6 g; Sodium: 680 mg

Winter Squash and Greens Couscous

Prep time: 15 min | Cook time: 30 min | Serving: 4

INGREDIENTS

- *1 small winter squash (such as butternut or acorn), peeled, seeded, and diced*
- *2 tablespoons olive oil*
- *Salt and black pepper, to taste*
- *1 cup whole wheat couscous*
- *1 1/2 cups vegetable broth or water*
- *2 cups mixed greens (such as spinach, kale, or Swiss chard), chopped*
- *1/4 cup dried cranberries or raisins*
- *1/4 cup chopped walnuts or pecans (optional)*
- *2 tablespoons balsamic vinegar*
- *2 tablespoons maple syrup or honey*
- *1/4 teaspoon ground cinnamon*
- *1/4 teaspoon ground nutmeg*

1) Preheat the oven to 400°F (200°C). Place the diced winter squash on a baking sheet. Drizzle with 1 tablespoon of olive oil and season with salt and black pepper to taste. Toss to coat evenly. Roast in the preheated oven for 20-25 minutes or until the squash is tender and lightly caramelized.

2) While the squash is roasting, prepare the couscous. In a medium saucepan, bring the vegetable broth or water to a boil. Stir in the couscous, cover, and remove from heat. Let it sit for 5 minutes, then fluff with a fork.

3) In a large skillet, heat the remaining tablespoon of olive oil over medium heat. Add the mixed greens and sauté for 2-3 minutes or until wilted.

4) Add the cooked couscous to the skillet with the greens. Stir in the roasted winter squash, dried cranberries or raisins, and chopped nuts (if using).

5) In a small bowl, whisk together the balsamic vinegar, maple syrup or honey, ground cinnamon, and ground nutmeg. Pour the dressing over the couscous mixture and toss everything together until well combined.

6) Cook for an additional 2-3 minutes, stirring occasionally until heated through.

7) Serve the Winter Squash and Greens Couscous warm as a delicious and nutritious main dish or side.

NUTRITION
Cal 320; Fat 8 g; Carb 60 g;
Protein 10 g; Fiber: 8 g; Sodium: 580 mg

Couscous Stuffed Bell Peppers

| Prep time: 15 min | Cook time 25 min | Serving: 2 |

INGREDIENTS

- *2 bell peppers, any color, halved and seeds removed*
- *1/2 cup couscous*
- *1 cup cooked chickpeas*
- *1/2 cup diced tomatoes*
- *1 cup chopped spinach*
- *1/4 cup crumbled feta cheese*
- *1/2 teaspoon ground cumin*
- *2 tablespoons olive oil*
- *Salt and black pepper, to taste*
- *Fresh parsley, chopped for garnish (optional)*

1) Preheat the oven to 375°F (190°C).
2) Cook the couscous according to package instructions. Fluff with a fork and set aside to cool slightly.
3) In a large mixing bowl, combine the cooked couscous, cooked chickpeas, diced tomatoes, chopped spinach, crumbled feta cheese, and ground cumin. Season with salt and black pepper to taste. Mix until well combined.
4) Place the halved bell peppers on a baking sheet, cut side up. Spoon the couscous mixture evenly into each bell pepper half.
5) Drizzle the stuffed bell peppers with olive oil.
6) Bake in the preheated oven for 20-25 minutes or until the peppers are tender and the filling is heated through.
7) Remove from the oven and garnish with chopped fresh parsley, if desired, before serving.

NUTRITION

Cal 380; Fat 15 g; Carb 50 g; Protein 12 g; Fiber: 10 g; Sodium: 580 mg

Grilled Vegetable Couscous Bowl

Prep time: 15 min | Cook time: 15 min | Serving: 2

INGREDIENTS

- *1 zucchini, sliced lengthwise*
- *1 red bell pepper, seeded, and quartered*
- *1 small eggplant, sliced into rounds*
- *1 cup cherry tomatoes*
- *1 cup couscous, cooked according to package instructions*
- *2 tablespoons fresh basil leaves, chopped*
- *Zest of 1 lemon*
- *Balsamic glaze for drizzling*
- *Salt and black pepper, to taste*
- *Olive oil for grilling*

1) Preheat the grill to medium-high heat.
2) Drizzle olive oil over the zucchini, bell pepper, eggplant, and cherry tomatoes. Season with salt and black pepper.
3) Grill the vegetables until they are charred and tender, about 4-5 minutes per side for the zucchini, bell pepper, and eggplant, and about 2-3 minutes for the cherry tomatoes. Remove from the grill and set aside.
4) In a large mixing bowl, combine the cooked couscous, grilled vegetables (cut into bite-sized pieces if desired), chopped fresh basil, and lemon zest. Toss gently to combine.
5) Divide the couscous and grilled vegetable mixture between two bowls.
6) Drizzle each bowl with balsamic glaze.

NUTRITION

Cal 320; Fat 8 g; Carb 60 g;
Protein 10 g; Fiber: 8 g; Sodium: 520 mg

Mediterranean Couscous Soup

| Prep time: 10 min | Cook time 20 min | Serving: 2 |

INGREDIENTS

- *1 cup cooked couscous*
- *3 cups vegetable broth*
- *1 can (14.5 oz) diced tomatoes*
- *1 carrot, diced*
- *1 celery stalk, diced*
- *1/2 onion, diced*
- *2 cloves garlic, minced*
- *1 handful spinach leaves*
- *1 teaspoon dried oregano*
- *1 teaspoon dried thyme*
- *Salt and black pepper, to taste*
- *Olive oil for sautéing*

1) In a pot, heat a drizzle of olive oil over medium heat.
2) Add diced onions, carrots, and celery to the pot. Sauté for about 5 minutes or until the vegetables are softened.
3) Add minced garlic to the pot and sauté for another minute until fragrant.
4) Pour in vegetable broth and diced tomatoes (with their juices) into the pot. Bring the mixture to a simmer.
5) Stir in cooked couscous, dried oregano, and dried thyme. Season with salt and black pepper to taste.
6) Allow the soup to simmer for about 10 minutes to allow the flavors to meld and the vegetables to become tender.
7) Add spinach leaves to the pot and simmer for another 2-3 minutes until the spinach is wilted.
8) Taste the soup and adjust seasoning if needed.

NUTRITION

Cal 250; Fat 3 g; Carb 50 g;
Protein 9 g; Fiber: 8 g; Sodium: 620 mg

Mediterranean Couscous Skillet

| Prep time: 10 min | Cook time 20 min | Serving: 2 |

INGREDIENTS

- *1 cup cooked couscous*
- *2 boneless, skinless chicken breasts, diced*
- *2 tablespoons olive oil*
- *2 cloves garlic, minced*
- *1/2 onion, diced*
- *1 bell pepper, diced (any color)*
- *1 can (14.5 oz) diced tomatoes, drained*
- *1/2 cup artichoke hearts, chopped*
- *1 handful spinach leaves*
- *1 teaspoon Italian seasoning*
- *Juice of 1 lemon*
- *Salt and black pepper, to taste*

1) In a large skillet, heat olive oil over medium heat.
2) Add diced chicken breast to the skillet and cook until browned and cooked through, about 6-8 minutes.
3) Add minced garlic, diced onion, and diced bell pepper to the skillet. Sauté for another 3-4 minutes until the vegetables are softened.
4) Stir in cooked couscous, drained diced tomatoes, chopped artichoke hearts, and spinach leaves. Cook for 2-3 minutes until the spinach is wilted.
5) Season the skillet with Italian seasoning, lemon juice, salt, and black pepper. Stir well to combine all ingredients.
6) Cook for another 2-3 minutes to allow the flavors to meld together.
7) Taste and adjust seasoning if needed.

NUTRITION
Cal 380; Fat 10 g; Carb 45 g;
Protein 30 g; Fiber: 8 g; Sodium: 680 mg

Greek Couscous Patties

| Prep time: 15 min | Cook time 10 min | Serving: 2 |

INGREDIENTS

- *1 cup cooked couscous*
- *1/4 cup crumbled feta cheese*
- *1/4 cup chopped spinach*
- *2 green onions, finely chopped*
- *1 large egg, beaten*
- *Salt and black pepper, to taste*
- *2 tablespoons olive oil for frying*
- *Tzatziki sauce for serving*

1) In a large mixing bowl, combine cooked couscous, crumbled feta cheese, chopped spinach, chopped green onions, and beaten egg. Season with salt and black pepper to taste. Mix well until all ingredients are evenly combined.
2) Using your hands, shape the mixture into patties, about 2 inches in diameter and 1/2 inch thick.
3) Heat olive oil in a large skillet over medium heat.
4) Once the skillet is hot, carefully place the couscous patties in the skillet, making sure not to overcrowd the pan. Cook in batches if necessary.
5) Pan-fry the patties for 3-4 minutes on each side or until golden brown and crispy.
6) Once cooked, transfer the patties to a plate lined with paper towels to drain any excess oil.
7) Serve the Greek Couscous Patties hot with tzatziki sauce for dipping.

NUTRITION

Cal 280; Fat 10 g; Carb 35 g; Protein 12 g; Fiber: 5 g; Sodium: 520 mg

SIDE DISHES

Couscous with Eggplant and Tomatoes

Prep time: 10 min	Cook time 20 min	Serving: 2

INGREDIENTS

- *1 cup couscous*
- *1 1/4 cups water or vegetable broth*
- *1 small eggplant, diced*
- *1 tablespoon olive oil*
- *2 cloves garlic, minced*
- *1 cup cherry tomatoes, halved*
- *1 tablespoon tomato paste*
- *1 teaspoon dried oregano*
- *Salt and black pepper, to taste*
- *Fresh parsley, chopped for garnish (optional)*

1) In a medium saucepan, bring water or vegetable broth to a boil. Stir in couscous, cover, and remove from heat. Let it sit for 5 minutes, then fluff with a fork.

2) While the couscous is cooking, heat olive oil in a large skillet over medium heat. Add diced eggplant and cook for about 5 minutes, stirring occasionally until softened.

3) Add minced garlic to the skillet and cook for another minute until fragrant.

4) Stir in cherry tomatoes, tomato paste, and dried oregano. Cook for 5-7 minutes or until the tomatoes have softened and released their juices, and the sauce has thickened slightly.

5) Season the eggplant and tomato mixture with salt and black pepper to taste.

6) Fluff the cooked couscous with a fork and transfer it to the skillet with the eggplant and tomatoes. Stir well to combine all ingredients.

7) Cook for another 2-3 minutes, stirring occasionally until everything is heated through.

8) Serve the Couscous with Eggplant and Tomatoes hot, garnished with chopped fresh parsley if desired.

NUTRITION

Cal 290; Fat 8 g; Carb 50 g;
Protein 7 g; Fiber: 6 g; Sodium: 480 mg

Bulgur with Eggplant, Zucchini, Tomatoes, and Mushrooms

| Prep time: 10 min | Cook time 20 min | Serving: 2 |

INGREDIENTS

- *1/2 cup bulgur wheat*
- *1 cup water or vegetable broth*
- *1 small eggplant, diced*
- *1 small zucchini, diced*
- *1 cup cherry tomatoes, halved*
- *1 cup mushrooms, sliced*
- *2 tablespoons olive oil*
- *2 cloves garlic, minced*
- *1 teaspoon dried oregano*
- *Salt and black pepper, to taste*
- *Fresh parsley, chopped for garnish (optional)*

1) Rinse the bulgur wheat under cold water and drain well.
2) In a medium saucepan, bring water or vegetable broth to a boil. Stir in bulgur wheat, cover, and simmer for 15-20 minutes or until the bulgur is tender and the liquid is absorbed. Remove from heat and let it sit, covered, for 5 minutes. Fluff with a fork.
3) While the bulgur is cooking, heat olive oil in a large skillet over medium heat. Add minced garlic and sauté for 1 minute until fragrant.
4) Add diced eggplant and zucchini to the skillet. Cook for about 5 minutes, stirring occasionally, until they start to soften.
5) Stir in cherry tomatoes and sliced mushrooms. Cook for another 5-7 minutes or until all the vegetables are tender and the tomatoes have released their juices.
6) Season the vegetable mixture with dried oregano, salt, and black pepper to taste. Stir well to combine.
7) Add the cooked bulgur to the skillet with the vegetables. Stir until everything is evenly combined and heated through.
8) Taste and adjust seasoning if needed.
9) Serve the Bulgur with Eggplant, Zucchini, Tomatoes, and Mushrooms hot, garnished with chopped fresh parsley if desired.

NUTRITION
Cal 320; Fat 8 g; Carb 55 g;
Protein 10 g; Fiber: 12 g; Sodium: 480 mg

Brown Rice with Zucchini and Spinach

| Prep time: 10 min | Cook time 30 min | Serving: 2 |

INGREDIENTS

- *1 cup brown rice*
- *2 cups water or vegetable broth*
- *1 medium zucchini, diced*
- *2 cups fresh spinach leaves*
- *2 cloves garlic, minced*
- *2 tablespoons olive oil*
- *Salt and black pepper, to taste*
- *Lemon wedges for serving (optional)*
- *Fresh parsley, chopped for garnish (optional)*

1) Rinse the brown rice under cold water and drain well.
2) In a medium saucepan, combine brown rice and water or vegetable broth. Bring to a boil, then reduce heat to low, cover, and simmer for 25-30 minutes or until the rice is tender and the liquid is absorbed. Remove from heat and let it sit, covered, for 5 minutes. Fluff with a fork.
3) While the rice is cooking, heat olive oil in a large skillet over medium heat. Add minced garlic and sauté for 1 minute until fragrant.
4) Add diced zucchini to the skillet. Cook for about 5 minutes, stirring occasionally until the zucchini starts to soften.
5) Stir in fresh spinach leaves and cook for another 2-3 minutes or until the spinach is wilted.
6) Season the zucchini and spinach mixture with salt and black pepper to taste. Stir well to combine.
7) Add the cooked brown rice to the skillet with the zucchini and spinach. Stir until everything is evenly combined and heated through.
8) Taste and adjust seasoning if needed.
9) Serve the Brown Rice with Zucchini and Spinach hot, garnished with chopped fresh parsley and lemon wedges if desired.

NUTRITION

Cal 240; Fat 4 g; Carb 48 g;
Protein 8 g; Fiber: 6 g; Sodium: 280 mg

Couscous with Zucchini, Green Peas, and Sweet Peppers

| Prep time: 10 min | Cook time 15 min | Serving: 2 |

INGREDIENTS

- *1 cup couscous*
- *1 1/4 cups water or vegetable broth*
- *1 medium zucchini, diced*
- *1/2 cup frozen green peas*
- *1 sweet pepper (any color), diced*
- *2 tablespoons olive oil*
- *2 cloves garlic, minced*
- *1/2 teaspoon paprika*
- *Salt and black pepper, to taste*
- *Fresh parsley, chopped for garnish (optional)*

1) In a medium saucepan, bring water or vegetable broth to a boil. Stir in couscous, cover, and remove from heat. Let it sit for 5 minutes, then fluff with a fork.
2) While the couscous is cooking, heat olive oil in a large skillet over medium heat. Add minced garlic and sauté for 1 minute until fragrant.
3) Add diced zucchini and sweet pepper to the skillet. Cook for about 5 minutes, stirring occasionally until the vegetables start to soften.
4) Stir in frozen green peas and continue to cook for another 2-3 minutes until the peas are heated through.
5) Season the vegetable mixture with paprika, salt, and black pepper to taste. Stir well to combine.
6) Fluff the cooked couscous with a fork and transfer it to the skillet with the vegetables. Stir until everything is evenly combined.
7) Cook for another 2-3 minutes, stirring occasionally until everything is heated through.
8) Taste and adjust seasoning if needed.
9) Serve the Couscous with Zucchini, Green Peas, and Sweet Peppers hot, garnished with chopped fresh parsley if desired.

NUTRITION
Cal 260; Fat 4 g; Carb 50 g;
Protein 9 g; Fiber: 6 g; Sodium: 280 mg

Couscous with Vegetables and Cheese

| Prep time: 10 min | Cook time 15 min | Serving: 2 |

INGREDIENTS

- *1 cup couscous*
- *1 1/4 cups water or vegetable broth*
- *1 tablespoon olive oil*
- *1 small onion, finely chopped*
- *1 bell pepper (any color), diced*
- *1 zucchini, diced*
- *1 cup cherry tomatoes, halved*
- *2 cloves garlic, minced*
- *1 teaspoon dried oregano*
- *Salt and black pepper, to taste*
- *1/2 cup crumbled feta cheese or shredded mozzarella cheese*
- *Fresh parsley, chopped for garnish (optional)*

1) In a medium saucepan, bring water or vegetable broth to a boil. Stir in couscous, cover, and remove from heat. Let it sit for 5 minutes, then fluff with a fork.
2) While the couscous is cooking, heat olive oil in a large skillet over medium heat. Add minced garlic and sauté for 1 minute until fragrant.
3) Add chopped onion to the skillet and cook for 2-3 minutes until translucent.
4) Add diced bell pepper and zucchini to the skillet. Cook for about 5 minutes, stirring occasionally until the vegetables start to soften.
5) Stir in cherry tomatoes and dried oregano. Cook for another 2-3 minutes or until the tomatoes are slightly softened.
6) Season the vegetable mixture with salt and black pepper to taste. Stir well to combine.
7) Fluff the cooked couscous with a fork and transfer it to the skillet with the vegetables. Stir until everything is evenly combined.
8) Sprinkle crumbled feta cheese or shredded mozzarella cheese over the couscous and vegetables. Cover the skillet and let it sit for a minute or two to allow the cheese to melt slightly.
9) Serve the Couscous with Vegetables and Cheese hot, garnished with chopped fresh parsley if desired.

NUTRITION

Cal 330; Fat 12 g; Carb 45 g;
Protein 12 g; Fiber: 6 g; Sodium: 540 mg

Quinoa with Spinach in Creamy Sauce

| Prep time: 5 min | Cook time 20 min | Serving: 2 |

INGREDIENTS

- *1/2 cup quinoa*
- *1 cup water or vegetable broth*
- *2 cups fresh spinach leaves*
- *2 tablespoons olive oil*
- *2 cloves garlic, minced*
- *1/2 onion, finely chopped*
- *1 tablespoon all-purpose flour*
- *1 cup milk (or non-dairy milk for a vegan option)*
- *1/4 cup grated Parmesan cheese (or nutritional yeast for a vegan option)*
- *Salt and black pepper, to taste*
- *Pinch of nutmeg (optional)*
- *Fresh parsley, chopped for garnish (optional)*

1) Rinse the quinoa under cold water and drain well.
2) In a medium saucepan, combine quinoa, and water or vegetable broth. Bring to a boil, then reduce heat to low, cover, and simmer for 15-20 minutes or until the quinoa is tender and the liquid is absorbed. Remove from heat and let it sit, covered, for 5 minutes. Fluff with a fork.
3) While the quinoa is cooking, heat olive oil in a large skillet over medium heat. Add minced garlic and sauté for 1 minute until fragrant.
4) Add chopped onion to the skillet and cook for 2-3 minutes until translucent.
5) Sprinkle all-purpose flour over the onions and garlic. Stir well to combine and cook for another minute.
6) Slowly pour in the milk, whisking continuously to prevent lumps from forming. Cook until the mixture thickens, about 3-5 minutes.
7) Stir in grated Parmesan cheese (or nutritional yeast) until melted and smooth. Season with salt, black pepper, and a pinch of nutmeg if using.
8) Add fresh spinach leaves to the skillet and cook for 2-3 minutes or until wilted.

9) Fluff the cooked quinoa with a fork and add it to the skillet with the creamy spinach sauce. Stir until everything is evenly combined and heated through.

10) Taste and adjust seasoning if needed.

11) Serve the Quinoa with Spinach in Creamy Sauce hot, garnished with chopped fresh parsley if desired.

NUTRITION
Cal 320; Fat 12 g; Carb 45 g;
Protein 12 g; Fiber: 6 g; Sodium: 460 mg

Spinach Casserole with Two Types of Cheese

Prep time: 10 min	Cook time 25 min	Serving: 2

INGREDIENTS

- *1 tablespoon olive oil*
- *2 cloves garlic, minced*
- *1/2 onion, finely chopped*
- *4 cups fresh spinach leaves*
- *1/4 cup grated Parmesan cheese*
- *1/4 cup crumbled feta cheese*
- *2 eggs, beaten*
- *1/2 cup Greek yogurt*
- *Salt and black pepper, to taste*
- *Pinch of nutmeg (optional)*
- *Fresh parsley, chopped for garnish (optional)*

1) Preheat your oven to 350°F (175°C). Grease a small baking dish with olive oil and set aside.
2) In a large skillet, heat olive oil over medium heat. Add minced garlic and chopped onion, and sauté for 2-3 minutes until softened.
3) Add fresh spinach leaves to the skillet and cook, stirring occasionally until wilted, about 2-3 minutes.
4) Remove the skillet from heat and transfer the spinach mixture to a mixing bowl.
5) Add grated Parmesan cheese, crumbled feta cheese, beaten eggs, and Greek yogurt to the bowl with the spinach. Season with salt, black pepper, and a pinch of nutmeg if desired. Stir until all ingredients are well combined.
6) Pour the spinach mixture into the greased baking dish, spreading it out evenly.
7) Bake in the preheated oven for 20-25 minutes or until the top is golden brown and the casserole is set.
8) Once baked, remove the casserole from the oven and let it cool for a few minutes before serving.
9) Garnish with chopped fresh parsley if desired, and serve hot.

NUTRITION
Cal 280; Fat 18 g; Carb 10 g;
Protein 20 g; Fiber: 3 g; Sodium: 520 mg

Warm Salad with Quinoa and Vegetables

Prep time: 10 min	Cook time 20 min	Serving: 2

INGREDIENTS

- *1/2 cup quinoa*
- *1 cup water or vegetable broth*
- *2 tablespoons olive oil*
- *2 cloves garlic, minced*
- *1 small red onion, thinly sliced*
- *1 bell pepper (any color), thinly sliced*
- *1 zucchini, halved lengthwise, and sliced*
- *1 cup cherry tomatoes, halved*
- *2 cups fresh spinach leaves*
- *1 tablespoon balsamic vinegar*
- *Salt and black pepper, to taste*
- *Crushed red pepper flakes, to taste (optional)*
- *Fresh basil leaves, chopped for garnish (optional)*
- *Crumbled feta cheese for garnish (optional)*

1) Rinse the quinoa under cold water and drain well.

2) In a medium saucepan, combine quinoa, and water or vegetable broth. Bring to a boil, then reduce heat to low, cover, and simmer for 15-20 minutes or until the quinoa is tender and the liquid is absorbed. Remove from heat and let it sit, covered, for 5 minutes. Fluff with a fork.

3) While the quinoa is cooking, heat olive oil in a large skillet over medium heat. Add minced garlic and sauté for 1 minute until fragrant.

4) Add thinly sliced red onion and bell pepper to the skillet. Cook for about 3-4 minutes until softened.

5) Add sliced zucchini to the skillet and cook for another 3-4 minutes until tender.

6) Stir in cherry tomatoes and fresh spinach leaves. Cook for 1-2 minutes until the spinach wilts and the tomatoes are slightly softened.

7) Add the cooked quinoa to the skillet with the vegetables. Drizzle with balsamic vinegar and toss everything together until well combined.

8) Season with salt, black pepper, and crushed red pepper flakes to taste, if using.

9) Divide the warm salad between serving plates.
10) Garnish with chopped fresh basil leaves and crumbled feta cheese, if desired.

NUTRITION
Cal 320; Fat 12 g; Carb 45 g;
Protein 10 g; Fiber: 8 g; Sodium: 480 mg

Bulgur and Quinoa Porridge with Onions

Prep time: 5 min	Cook time: 20 min	Serving: 2

INGREDIENTS

- *1/4 cup bulgur wheat*
- *1/4 cup quinoa*
- *1 cup water or vegetable broth*
- *1 tablespoon olive oil*
- *1 small onion, finely chopped*
- *2 cloves garlic, minced*
- *1/2 teaspoon ground cumin*
- *Salt and black pepper, to taste*
- *Fresh parsley, chopped for garnish (optional)*

1) Rinse the bulgur wheat and quinoa under cold water and drain well.
2) In a small saucepan, combine bulgur wheat, quinoa, and water or vegetable broth. Bring to a boil, then reduce heat to low, cover, and simmer for 15-20 minutes or until the grains are tender and the liquid is absorbed. Remove from heat and let it sit, covered, for 5 minutes. Fluff with a fork.
3) While the grains are cooking, heat olive oil in a skillet over medium heat. Add chopped onion and sauté for 3-4 minutes until softened.
4) Add minced garlic to the skillet and sauté for another minute until fragrant.
5) Stir in ground cumin and cook for another minute to toast the spices.
6) Add the cooked bulgur and quinoa to the skillet with the onions and garlic. Mix well to combine.
7) Season with salt and black pepper to taste.
8) Cook for an additional 2-3 minutes, stirring occasionally until everything is heated through.

NUTRITION

Cal 260; Fat 8 g; Carb 40 g;
Protein 10 g; Fiber: 6 g; Sodium: 480 mg

Bulgur and Orzo Pasta with Vegetables

| Prep time: 10 min | Cook time: 20 min | Serving: 2 |

INGREDIENTS

- *1/2 cup bulgur wheat*
- *1/2 cup orzo pasta*
- *1 cup water or vegetable broth*
- *2 tablespoons olive oil*
- *2 cloves garlic, minced*
- *1 small onion, finely chopped*
- *1 bell pepper (any color), diced*
- *1 zucchini, diced*
- *1 cup cherry tomatoes, halved*
- *1 teaspoon dried oregano*
- *Salt and black pepper, to taste*
- *Fresh parsley, chopped for garnish (optional)*

1) Rinse the bulgur wheat and orzo pasta under cold water and drain well.
2) In a medium saucepan, combine bulgur wheat, orzo pasta, and water or vegetable broth. Bring to a boil, then reduce heat to low, cover, and simmer for 10-12 minutes or until the grains and pasta are tender and the liquid is absorbed. Remove from heat and let it sit, covered, for 5 minutes. Fluff with a fork.
3) While the grains and pasta are cooking, heat olive oil in a large skillet over medium heat. Add minced garlic and chopped onion, and sauté for 2-3 minutes until softened.
4) Add diced bell pepper and zucchini to the skillet. Cook for about 5 minutes, stirring occasionally until the vegetables start to soften.
5) Stir in cherry tomatoes and dried oregano. Cook for another 2-3 minutes or until the tomatoes are slightly softened.
6) Add the cooked bulgur and orzo pasta to the skillet with the vegetables. Stir until everything is evenly combined.
7) Season with salt and black pepper to taste. Stir well to incorporate the seasoning.
8) Cook for another 2-3 minutes, stirring occasionally until everything is heated through.
9) Serve the Bulgur and Orzo Pasta with Vegetables hot, garnished with chopped fresh parsley if desired.

NUTRITION

Cal 320; Fat 8 g; Carb 55 g;
Protein 10 g; Fiber: 8 g; Sodium: 480 mg

SALAD

Quinoa Tabbouleh Salad

Prep time: 15 min	Cook time: 15 min	Serving: 2

INGREDIENTS

- *1/2 cup quinoa*
- *1 cup water*
- *1 cup fresh parsley, finely chopped*
- *1/4 cup fresh mint leaves, finely chopped*
- *1/2 cucumber, diced*
- *1 tomato, diced*
- *2 green onions, thinly sliced*
- *2 tablespoons olive oil*
- *1 lemon, juiced*
- *Salt and black pepper, to taste*

1) Rinse the quinoa under cold water using a fine-mesh sieve. In a small saucepan, combine the rinsed quinoa and water. Bring to a boil over medium-high heat.

2) Reduce the heat to low, cover, and simmer for 15 minutes or until the quinoa is tender and the water is absorbed. Remove from heat and let it cool slightly.

3) In a large mixing bowl, combine the cooked quinoa, finely chopped parsley, finely chopped mint leaves, diced cucumber, diced tomato, and thinly sliced green onions.

4) In a small bowl, whisk together the olive oil and lemon juice to make the dressing.

5) Pour the dressing over the quinoa tabbouleh salad and toss to combine, ensuring the ingredients are evenly coated.

6) Season with salt and black pepper to taste.

7) Serve the Quinoa Tabbouleh Salad immediately, or refrigerate for at least 30 minutes to allow the flavors to meld before serving.

NUTRITION
Cal 280; Fat 14 g; Carb 34 g;
Protein 7 g; Fiber: 5 g; Sodium: 15 mg

Mediterranean Zoodle Salad

Prep time: 15 min	Cook time 0 min	Serving: 2

INGREDIENTS

- *2 medium zucchini, spiralized into "zoodles"*
- *1 cup cherry tomatoes, halved*
- *1/2 cup diced bell peppers (any color)*
- *1/4 cup sliced olives (Kalamata or black)*
- *1/4 cup crumbled feta cheese*
- *2 tablespoons chopped fresh basil*
- *For the vinaigrette:*
- *2 tablespoons extra virgin olive oil*
- *1 tablespoon red wine vinegar*
- *1 clove garlic, minced*
- *1/2 teaspoon Italian seasoning*
- *Salt and black pepper, to taste*

1) In a large mixing bowl, combine the spiralized zucchini "zoodles", halved cherry tomatoes, diced bell peppers, sliced olives, crumbled feta cheese, and chopped fresh basil.

2) In a small bowl, whisk together the extra virgin olive oil, red wine vinegar, minced garlic, Italian seasoning, salt, and black pepper to make the vinaigrette.

3) Pour the vinaigrette over the zoodle salad and toss until all ingredients are evenly coated.

4) Serve the Mediterranean Zoodle Salad immediately, or refrigerate for at least 30 minutes to allow the flavors to meld before serving.

NUTRITION
Cal 210; Fat 16 g; Carb 14 g;
Protein 6 g; Fiber: 4 g; Sodium: 330 mg

Shrimp and Avocado Salad

Prep time: 15 min	Cook time 5 min	Serving: 2

INGREDIENTS

- *8 ounces shrimp, peeled, and deveined*
- *4 cups mixed greens*
- *1 avocado, sliced*
- *1/2 red bell pepper, diced*
- *1/2 cucumber, diced*
- *1/2 cup cherry tomatoes, halved*
- *1/4 cup crumbled goat cheese*
- **For the vinaigrette:**
- *2 tablespoons extra virgin olive oil*
- *1 tablespoon lemon juice*
- *1 teaspoon Dijon mustard*
- *Salt and black pepper, to taste*

1) Heat a grill or skillet over medium-high heat. Cook the shrimp for 2-3 minutes on each side until they are pink and cooked through.

2) In a large mixing bowl, combine the mixed greens, sliced avocado, diced red bell pepper, diced cucumber, cherry tomatoes, and crumbled goat cheese.

3) In a small bowl, whisk together the extra virgin olive oil, lemon juice, Dijon mustard, salt, and black pepper to make the vinaigrette.

4) Drizzle the vinaigrette over the salad and toss until all ingredients are evenly coated.

5) Divide the salad between two plates and top each portion with grilled or sautéed shrimp.

NUTRITION
Cal 370; Fat 25 g; Carb 18 g;
Protein 24 g; Fiber: 9 g; Sodium: 460 mg

Mediterranean Chickpea and Quinoa Salad

| Prep time: 10 min | Cook time 15 min | Serving: 2 |

INGREDIENTS

- *1/2 cup quinoa*
- *1 cup water or vegetable broth*
- *1 cup cooked chickpeas (canned or cooked from dry)*
- *1 cup cherry tomatoes, halved*
- *1/2 cucumber, diced*
- *1/4 cup red onion, finely chopped*
- *1/4 cup Kalamata olives, pitted and sliced*
- *2 tablespoons fresh parsley, chopped*
- *2 tablespoons fresh mint leaves, chopped*
- *2 tablespoons extra-virgin olive oil*
- *1 tablespoon lemon juice*
- *1 clove garlic, minced*
- *Salt and black pepper, to taste*
- *Crumbled feta cheese for garnish (optional)*

1) Rinse the quinoa under cold water and drain well.
2) In a small saucepan, combine quinoa and water or vegetable broth. Bring to a boil, then reduce heat to low, cover, and simmer for 15 minutes or until the quinoa is tender and the liquid is absorbed. Remove from heat and let it sit, covered, for 5 minutes. Fluff with a fork and let it cool slightly.
3) In a large mixing bowl, combine the cooked quinoa, chickpeas, cherry tomatoes, cucumber, red onion, Kalamata olives, fresh parsley, and fresh mint leaves.
4) In a small bowl, whisk together the extra-virgin olive oil, lemon juice, minced garlic, salt, and black pepper to make the dressing.
5) Pour the dressing over the salad ingredients in the mixing bowl and toss until everything is well coated.
6) Taste and adjust seasoning if needed.
7) Divide the Mediterranean Chickpea and Quinoa Salad between two serving plates or bowls.
8) Garnish with crumbled feta cheese, if desired.
9) Serve the salad immediately, or refrigerate for at least 30 minutes to allow the flavors to meld before serving.

NUTRITION
Cal 380; Fat 15 g; Carb 50 g;
Protein 14 g; Fiber: 12 g; Sodium: 520 mg

Green Mediterranean Salad

| Prep time: 10 min | Cook time 0 min | Serving: 2 |

INGREDIENTS

- 4 cups mixed salad greens (such as lettuce, spinach, and arugula)
- 1 cup cherry tomatoes, halved
- 1/2 cucumber, sliced
- 1/4 red onion, thinly sliced
- 1/4 cup Kalamata olives, pitted
- 2 tablespoons crumbled feta cheese
- 2 tablespoons extra-virgin olive oil
- 1 tablespoon red wine vinegar
- 1 clove garlic, minced
- 1 teaspoon dried oregano
- Salt and black pepper, to taste
- Lemon wedges, for serving (optional)

1) In a large salad bowl, combine mixed salad greens, cherry tomatoes, cucumber slices, red onion slices, and Kalamata olives.
2) In a small bowl, whisk together extra-virgin olive oil, red wine vinegar, minced garlic, dried oregano, salt, and black pepper to make the dressing.
3) Pour the dressing over the salad ingredients.
4) Toss the salad gently until everything is evenly coated with the dressing.
5) Sprinkle crumbled feta cheese over the top of the salad.
6) Serve the Tossed Green Mediterranean Salad immediately, with lemon wedges on the side for squeezing over the salad, if desired.

NUTRITION
Cal 160; Fat 12 g; Carb 10 g;
Protein 4 g; Fiber: 4 g; Sodium: 280 mg

Beet and Walnut Salad

Prep time: 10 min | Cook time: 40 min | Serving: 2

INGREDIENTS

- *2 medium beets, cooked, peeled, and sliced*
- *1/4 cup walnuts, chopped, and toasted*
- *2 cups mixed salad greens (such as lettuce, spinach, and arugula)*
- *1/4 cup crumbled feta cheese*
- *2 tablespoons extra-virgin olive oil*
- *1 tablespoon balsamic vinegar*
- *1 teaspoon Dijon mustard*
- *1 clove garlic, minced*
- *Salt and black pepper, to taste*

1) Preheat your oven to 400°F (200°C). Wrap each beet individually in aluminum foil and place them on a baking sheet. Roast in the preheated oven for about 40 minutes or until the beets are tender when pierced with a fork. Let them cool slightly, then peel and slice them.

2) While the beets are roasting, toast the chopped walnuts in a dry skillet over medium heat for 3-4 minutes or until fragrant and lightly browned. Remove from heat and let them cool.

3) In a large salad bowl, combine the mixed salad greens, sliced roasted beets, toasted walnuts, and crumbled feta cheese.

4) In a small bowl, whisk together the extra-virgin olive oil, balsamic vinegar, Dijon mustard, minced garlic, salt, and black pepper to make the dressing.

5) Drizzle the dressing over the salad ingredients.

6) Toss the salad gently until everything is evenly coated with the dressing.

NUTRITION

Cal 220; Fat 15 g; Carb 20 g;
Protein 5 g; Fiber: 5 g; Sodium: 160 mg

Cabbage and Carrot Salad

| Prep time: 10 min | Cook time 0 min | Serving: 2 |

INGREDIENTS

- *2 cups shredded green cabbage*
- *1 large carrot, grated*
- *2 tablespoons chopped fresh parsley*
- *2 tablespoons extra-virgin olive oil*
- *1 tablespoon lemon juice*
- *1 clove garlic, minced*
- *1/2 teaspoon honey or maple syrup (optional)*
- *Salt and black pepper, to taste*
- *1 tablespoon toasted sesame seeds for garnish (optional)*

1) In a large bowl, combine the shredded green cabbage, grated carrot, and chopped fresh parsley.

2) In a small bowl, whisk together the extra-virgin olive oil, lemon juice, minced garlic, honey or maple syrup (if using), salt, and black pepper to make the dressing.

3) Pour the dressing over the cabbage and carrot mixture.

4) Toss the salad gently until everything is evenly coated with the dressing.

5) Taste and adjust seasoning if needed.

6) Serve the Cabbage and Carrot Salad immediately, garnished with toasted sesame seeds if desired.

NUTRITION

Cal 90; Fat 6 g; Carb 10 g;
Protein 2 g; Fiber: 4 g; Sodium: 25 mg

Watermelon and Feta Salad

| Prep time: 10 min | Cook time: 0 min | Serving: 2 |

INGREDIENTS

- *2 cups cubed watermelon*
- *2 ounces feta cheese, crumbled*
- *2 tablespoons fresh mint leaves, chopped*
- *1 tablespoon extra-virgin olive oil*
- *1 tablespoon balsamic vinegar*
- *Salt and black pepper, to taste*
- *2 tablespoons chopped walnuts or pistachios for garnish (optional)*

1) In a large bowl, combine the cubed watermelon, crumbled feta cheese, and chopped fresh mint leaves.
2) In a small bowl, whisk together the extra-virgin olive oil and balsamic vinegar to make the dressing.
3) Drizzle the dressing over the watermelon and feta mixture.
4) Toss the salad gently until everything is evenly coated with the dressing.
5) Season with salt and black pepper to taste.
6) Serve the Watermelon and Feta Salad immediately, garnished with chopped walnuts or pistachios if desired.

NUTRITION

Cal 150; Fat 8 g; Carb 16 g; Protein 6 g; Fiber: 2 g; Sodium: 280 mg

Horta (Warm Greens Salad)

| Prep time: 10 min | Cook time 10 min | Serving: 2 |

INGREDIENTS

- *1 bunch of mixed greens (such as spinach, kale, or Swiss chard), washed, and chopped*
- *2 tablespoons extra-virgin olive oil*
- *2 cloves garlic, minced*
- *1/4 teaspoon red pepper flakes (optional)*
- *Juice of 1/2 lemon*
- *Salt and black pepper, to taste*
- *Crumbled feta cheese for garnish (optional)*
- *Toasted pine nuts or almonds for garnish (optional)*

1) In a large skillet, heat the olive oil over medium heat.
2) Add the minced garlic and red pepper flakes (if using) to the skillet. Sauté for 1-2 minutes until the garlic is fragrant.
3) Add the chopped greens to the skillet. Cook, stirring occasionally, for 5-7 minutes until the greens are wilted and tender.
4) Squeeze the lemon juice over the cooked greens and season with salt and black pepper to taste. Stir to combine.
5) Transfer the warm greens to a serving dish.
6) Garnish the Horta with crumbled feta cheese and toasted pine nuts or almonds, if desired.

NUTRITION
Cal 120; Fat 9 g; Carb 8 g;
Protein 3 g; Fiber: 4 g; Sodium: 360 mg

Zucchini and Ricotta Salad

Prep time: 10 min	Cook time: 5 min	Serving: 2

INGREDIENTS

- *2 medium zucchinis, thinly sliced*
- *1 tablespoon extra-virgin olive oil*
- *Salt and black pepper, to taste*
- *1/2 cup ricotta cheese*
- *Zest of 1 lemon*
- *1 tablespoon lemon juice*
- *2 tablespoons chopped fresh basil*
- *1 tablespoon chopped fresh mint*
- *2 tablespoons chopped walnuts, toasted (optional)*

1) Heat the olive oil in a large skillet over medium heat. Add the sliced zucchinis and cook for 3-4 minutes, stirring occasionally until they are tender and lightly browned. Season with salt and black pepper to taste. Remove from heat and let them cool slightly.

2) In a small bowl, combine the ricotta cheese, lemon zest, lemon juice, chopped basil, and chopped mint. Mix well to combine.

3) Arrange the cooked zucchini slices on a serving platter.

4) Spoon the ricotta mixture over the zucchini slices.

5) Sprinkle with toasted walnuts (if using).

6) Serve the Zucchini and Ricotta Salad immediately, or chill in the refrigerator for 30 minutes to allow the flavors to meld before serving.

NUTRITION
Cal 180; Fat 12 g; Carb 8 g;
Protein 10 g; Fiber: 2 g; Sodium: 190 mg

Sicilian Salad

Prep time: 10 min | Cook time: 0 min | Serving: 2

INGREDIENTS

- *2 tablespoons extra virgin olive oil*
- *1 tablespoon red wine vinegar*
- *2 medium tomatoes, sliced*
- *1/2 medium red onion, thinly sliced*
- *2 tablespoons capers, drained*
- *6 green olives, halved*
- *1 teaspoon dried oregano*
- *Pinch of fine sea salt*

1) In a small bowl, whisk together the extra virgin olive oil and red wine vinegar to make the dressing. Set aside.
2) On a serving platter, arrange the sliced tomatoes in a single layer.
3) Scatter the thinly sliced red onion over the tomatoes.
4) Sprinkle the capers and halved green olives over the tomatoes and onions.
5) Drizzle the prepared dressing over the salad.
6) Sprinkle dried oregano and a pinch of fine sea salt over the salad.
7) Serve the Sicilian Salad immediately as a refreshing appetizer or side dish.

NUTRITION

Cal 220; Fat 16 g; Carb 10 g;
Protein 6 g; Fiber: 2 g; Sodium: 220 mg

Citrus Avocado Salad

| Prep time: 10 min | Cook time 0 min | Serving: 2 |

INGREDIENTS

- *1 large avocado, peeled, pitted, and sliced*
- *2 oranges, peeled, and sliced*
- *1 grapefruit, peeled, and sliced*
- *1/4 red onion, thinly sliced*
- *2 tablespoons chopped fresh mint leaves*
- *2 tablespoons extra-virgin olive oil*
- *1 tablespoon balsamic vinegar*
- *Salt and black pepper, to taste*
- *Optional: toasted nuts or seeds for garnish (such as almonds or pumpkin seeds)*

1) Arrange the sliced avocado, oranges, and grapefruit on a serving platter.
2) Scatter the thinly sliced red onion over the citrus and avocado.
3) Sprinkle the chopped fresh mint leaves over the salad.
4) In a small bowl, whisk together the extra-virgin olive oil and balsamic vinegar to make the dressing.
5) Drizzle the dressing over the Citrus Avocado Salad.
6) Season with salt and black pepper to taste.
7) Optional: Garnish with toasted nuts or seeds for added crunch and flavor.

NUTRITION

Cal 220; Fat 18 g; Carb 15 g; Protein 3 g; Fiber: 9 g; Sodium: 10 mg

Italian Summer Vegetable Barley Salad

Prep time: 15 min	Cook time 30 min	Serving: 2

INGREDIENTS

- *1/2 cup pearl barley*
- *1 cup water or vegetable broth*
- *1 small zucchini, diced*
- *1 small yellow squash, diced*
- *1 cup cherry tomatoes, halved*
- *1/4 cup red onion, finely chopped*
- *2 tablespoons chopped fresh basil*
- *2 tablespoons chopped fresh parsley*
- *2 tablespoons extra-virgin olive oil*
- *1 tablespoon balsamic vinegar*
- *1 clove garlic, minced*
- *Salt and black pepper, to taste*
- *Grated Parmesan cheese for garnish (optional)*

1) Rinse the pearl barley under cold water and drain well.

2) In a medium saucepan, bring 1 cup of water or vegetable broth to a boil. Add the rinsed barley, reduce the heat to low, cover, and simmer for 25-30 minutes or until the barley is tender and the liquid is absorbed. Remove from heat and let it cool slightly.

3) In a large mixing bowl, combine the cooked barley, diced zucchini, diced yellow squash, halved cherry tomatoes, finely chopped red onion, chopped fresh basil, and chopped fresh parsley.

4) In a small bowl, whisk together the extra-virgin olive oil, balsamic vinegar, minced garlic, salt, and black pepper to make the dressing.

5) Pour the dressing over the barley and vegetable mixture.

6) Toss the salad gently until everything is evenly coated with the dressing.

7) Taste and adjust seasoning if needed.

8) Serve the, Italian Summer Vegetable Barley Salad immediately, garnished with grated Parmesan cheese if desired.

NUTRITION
Cal 220; Fat 7 g; Carb 35 g;
Protein 6 g; Fiber: 8 g; Sodium: 280 mg

Greek Chicken Gyro Salad

| Prep time: 15 min | Cook time: 15 min | Serving: 2 |

INGREDIENTS

- *For the Chicken:*
- *2 boneless, skinless chicken breasts*
- *1 tablespoon olive oil*
- *1 teaspoon dried oregano*
- *1 teaspoon garlic powder*
- *Salt and black pepper, to taste*
- *For the Salad:*
- *4 cups mixed salad greens (such as lettuce, spinach, and arugula)*
- *1 cucumber, thinly sliced*
- *1 cup cherry tomatoes, halved*
- *1/4 red onion, thinly sliced*
- *1/4 cup Kalamata olives, pitted*
- *2 ounces feta cheese, crumbled*
- *For the Dressing:*
- *2 tablespoons extra-virgin olive oil*
- *1 tablespoon red wine vinegar*
- *1 teaspoon dried oregano*
- *1 clove garlic, minced*
- *Salt and black pepper, to taste*

1) Preheat the grill or grill pan over medium-high heat.
2) In a small bowl, combine olive oil, dried oregano, garlic powder, salt, and black pepper. Rub the mixture over the chicken breasts.
3) Grill the chicken breasts for 6-8 minutes per side or until cooked through and no longer pink in the center. Remove from the grill and let them rest for a few minutes before slicing.
4) In a large salad bowl, combine the mixed salad greens, cucumber slices, cherry tomatoes, thinly sliced red onion, Kalamata olives, and crumbled feta cheese.
5) In a small bowl, whisk together the extra-virgin olive oil, red wine vinegar, dried oregano, minced garlic, salt, and black pepper to make the dressing.
6) Drizzle the dressing over the salad ingredients and toss to coat evenly.
7) Divide the salad mixture between two plates.
8) Slice the grilled chicken breasts and arrange them on top of the salads.

NUTRITION
Cal 320; Fat 15 g; Carb 15 g;
Protein 30 g; Fiber: 5 g; Sodium: 680 mg

Cauliflower and Farro Salad

Prep time: 15 min | Cook time: 20 min | Serving: 2

INGREDIENTS

- *1 cup farro, rinsed*
- *2 cups water or vegetable broth*
- *1 small head cauliflower, cut into small florets*
- *2 tablespoons olive oil*
- *1 teaspoon ground cumin*
- *1 teaspoon smoked paprika*
- *Salt and black pepper, to taste*
- *2 cups baby spinach leaves*
- *1/4 cup chopped fresh parsley*
- *1/4 cup chopped fresh mint*
- *1/4 cup crumbled feta cheese (optional)*
- *2 tablespoons lemon juice*
- *1 tablespoon balsamic vinegar*
- *1 clove garlic, minced*
- *2 tablespoons toasted pine nuts (optional)*

1) In a medium saucepan, bring the water or vegetable broth to a boil. Add the rinsed farro, reduce the heat to low, cover, and simmer for 20-25 minutes or until the farro is tender but still chewy. Drain any excess liquid and let it cool slightly.
2) Preheat the oven to 400°F (200°C). Line a baking sheet with parchment paper.
3) In a large bowl, toss the cauliflower florets with olive oil, ground cumin, smoked paprika, salt, and black pepper until evenly coated. Spread the cauliflower in a single layer on the prepared baking sheet.
4) Roast the cauliflower in the preheated oven for 20-25 minutes or until golden brown and tender, stirring halfway through cooking.
5) In a large mixing bowl, combine the cooked farro, roasted cauliflower, baby spinach leaves, chopped fresh parsley, and chopped fresh mint. If using, add crumbled feta cheese and toasted pine nuts.
6) In a small bowl, whisk together the lemon juice, balsamic vinegar, minced garlic, salt, and black pepper to make the dressing.
7) Drizzle the dressing over the salad ingredients and toss gently to coat.
8) Serve the Cauliflower and Farro Salad immediately, or refrigerate for 30 minutes to allow the flavors to meld before serving.

NUTRITION

Cal 280; Fat 10 g; Carb 38 g; Protein 9 g; Fiber: 8 g; Sodium: 380 mg

DESSERTS

Mediterranean Fruit Sorbet

Prep time: 5 min	Cook time: 0 min	Serving: 2

INGREDIENTS

- *1 cup frozen mango chunks*
- *1 cup frozen pineapple chunks*
- *1 cup frozen peach slices*
- *1/4 cup coconut water*

1) Place the frozen mango, pineapple, and peach chunks in a blender.
2) Add the coconut water to the blender.
3) Blend the ingredients on high speed until smooth and creamy, scraping down the sides of the blender as needed.
4) Once the mixture is smooth and resembles sorbet, stop blending.
5) Serve the Mediterranean Fruit Sorbet immediately in bowls or glasses.
6) Optionally, garnish with fresh mint leaves or a slice of lime for an extra burst of flavor.

NUTRITION
Cal 120; Fat 0 g; Carb 30 g;
Protein 1 g; Fiber: 4 g; Sodium: 10 mg

Italian Chocolate Coffee Cake

Prep time: 15 min	Cook time 35 min	Serving: 2

INGREDIENTS

- *1 and 1/2 cups all-purpose flour*
- *1/2 cup unsweetened cocoa powder*
- *1 teaspoon baking powder*
- *1/2 teaspoon baking soda*
- *1/4 teaspoon salt*
- *1/2 cup unsalted butter, softened*
- *1 cup granulated sugar*
- *2 large eggs*
- *1 teaspoon vanilla extract*
- *1/2 cup strong brewed coffee, cooled*
- *1/2 cup milk*
- *Powdered sugar for dusting (optional)*

1) Preheat the oven to 350°F (175°C). Grease and flour a 9-inch round cake pan.
2) In a medium bowl, sift together the all-purpose flour, cocoa powder, baking powder, baking soda, and salt. Set aside.
3) In a large mixing bowl, cream together the softened butter and granulated sugar until light and fluffy.
4) Beat in the eggs, one at a time until well combined. Stir in the vanilla extract.
5) Gradually add the dry ingredients to the wet ingredients, alternating with coffee and milk, beginning and ending with the dry ingredients. Mix until just combined.
6) Pour the batter into the prepared cake pan and spread it evenly with a spatula.
7) Bake in the preheated oven for 30-35 minutes or until a toothpick inserted into the center comes out clean.
8) Remove the cake from the oven and let it cool in the pan for 10 minutes before transferring it to a wire rack to cool completely.
9) Once cooled, dust the Italian Chocolate Coffee Cake with powdered sugar if desired.
10) Slice and serve the cake as a delicious dessert or treat, perfect for pairing with a cup of coffee or tea.

NUTRITION
Cal 280; Fat 12 g; Carb 38 g;
Protein 5 g; Fiber: 2 g; Sodium: 200 mg

Greek Almond Cookies

| Prep time: 15 min | Cook time 15 min | Serving: 2 |

INGREDIENTS

- *1 cup almond flour*
- *1 cup powdered sugar*
- *1/4 teaspoon almond extract*
- *1/4 teaspoon vanilla extract*
- *1 large egg white*
- *Pinch of salt*
- *Sliced almonds for garnish (optional)*

1) Preheat the oven to 325°F (160°C). Line a baking sheet with parchment paper.
2) In a mixing bowl, combine the almond flour and powdered sugar.
3) Add the almond extract, vanilla extract, and egg white to the dry ingredients. Mix until a dough forms.
4) If the dough is too sticky, you can add a little more almond flour until it reaches a workable consistency.
5) Pinch off small pieces of dough and roll them into balls about 1 inch in diameter. Place the balls on the prepared baking sheet, leaving some space between each cookie.
6) Flatten each ball slightly with the palm of your hand or the back of a fork. If desired, press a sliced almond into the center of each cookie for garnish.
7) Bake in the preheated oven for 12-15 minutes or until the cookies are set and lightly golden around the edges.
8) Remove the cookies from the oven and let them cool on the baking sheet for a few minutes before transferring them to a wire rack to cool completely.
9) Once cooled, store the Greek Almond Cookies in an airtight container at room temperature.

NUTRITION

Cal 80; Fat 4 g; Carb 10 g;
Protein 2 g; Fiber: 1 g; Sodium: 10 mg

Baked Pears with Ricotta and Honey

Prep time: 10 min | Cook time: 25 min | Serving: 2

INGREDIENTS

- *2 ripe pears*
- *1/2 cup ricotta cheese*
- *1 tablespoon honey*
- *1/2 teaspoon ground cinnamon*

1) Preheat your oven to 375°F (190°C). Line a baking dish with parchment paper or lightly grease it with butter.
2) Wash the pears and cut them in half lengthwise. Use a spoon to remove the seeds and create a hollow center in each pear half.
3) In a small bowl, mix together the ricotta cheese, honey, and ground cinnamon until well combined.
4) Spoon the ricotta mixture into the center of each pear half, filling it generously.
5) Place the stuffed pear halves in the prepared baking dish.
6) Bake in the preheated oven for about 20-25 minutes or until the pears are tender and the ricotta is bubbly and lightly golden on top.
7) Remove from the oven and let cool for a few minutes before serving.
8) Optionally, drizzle with additional honey and sprinkle with a pinch of cinnamon before serving.

NUTRITION

Cal 220; Fat 6 g; Carb 40 g;
Protein 7 g; Fiber: 6 g; Sodium: 45 mg

Fruit Skewers with Yogurt Dip

Prep time: 15 min | Cook time 0 min | Serving: 2

INGREDIENTS

- *1 cup strawberries, hulled, and halved*
- *1 kiwi, peeled, and sliced*
- *1 cup grapes (red or green), washed*
- *1 cup pineapple chunks*
- *1/2 cup Greek yogurt*
- *1 tablespoon honey (optional)*

1) Prepare the fruit by washing, peeling (if necessary), and cutting it into bite-sized chunks.
2) Thread the fruit chunks onto skewers, alternating the varieties for a colorful presentation.
3) In a small bowl, mix the Greek yogurt with honey, if using, until well combined.
4) Arrange the fruit skewers on a serving platter alongside the bowl of yogurt dip.
5) Serve the fruit skewers with the yogurt dip for dipping.
6) Enjoy the refreshing combination of sweet, juicy fruits with the creamy and slightly tangy yogurt dip.

NUTRITION
Cal 120; Fat 0 g; Carb 25 g;
Protein 6 g; Fiber: 4 g; Sodium: 20 mg

Greek Yogurt Bark with Berries

| Prep time: 10 min | Cook time 4 hours | Serving: 2 |

INGREDIENTS

- *1 cup Greek yogurt (plain or vanilla)*
- *1 tablespoon honey or maple syrup (optional, adjust to taste)*
- *1/2 cup mixed berries (such as strawberries, blueberries, raspberries)*
- *2 tablespoons chopped nuts or seeds (such as almonds, walnuts, or pumpkin seeds)*
- *1 tablespoon unsweetened coconut flakes (optional)*

1) Line a baking sheet or shallow dish with parchment paper.
2) In a mixing bowl, combine the Greek yogurt with honey or maple syrup if using, and mix well.
3) Spread the Greek yogurt mixture evenly onto the prepared baking sheet or dish, about 1/4 inch thick.
4) Sprinkle the mixed berries, chopped nuts or seeds, and unsweetened coconut flakes evenly over the Greek yogurt layer, pressing them gently into the yogurt.
5) Place the baking sheet or dish in the freezer and freeze for at least 4 hours or until the yogurt bark is completely frozen.
6) Once frozen, remove the bark from the freezer and break it into pieces using your hands or a knife.
7) Serve immediately as a refreshing snack or dessert.
8) Store any leftovers in an airtight container in the freezer.

NUTRITION
Cal 120; Fat 2 g; Carb 17 g;
Protein 8 g; Fiber: 3 g; Sodium: 35 mg

Greek Orange Honey Cake with Pistachios

Prep time: 15 min	Cook time 30 min	Serving: 2

INGREDIENTS

- *1/2 cup all-purpose flour*
- *1/4 cup almond flour*
- *1/4 cup granulated sugar*
- *1/2 teaspoon baking powder*
- *1/4 teaspoon baking soda*
- *Pinch of salt*
- *Zest of 1 orange*
- *1/4 cup Greek yogurt*
- *2 tablespoons olive oil*
- *2 tablespoons honey*
- *1 large egg*
- *1/4 cup freshly squeezed orange juice*
- *2 tablespoons chopped pistachios*
- *Extra honey for drizzling (optional)*

1) Preheat your oven to 350°F (175°C). Grease a small baking dish or two ramekins with olive oil or non-stick cooking spray.
2) In a mixing bowl, whisk together the all-purpose flour, almond flour, granulated sugar, baking powder, baking soda, salt, and orange zest.
3) In a separate bowl, whisk together the Greek yogurt, olive oil, honey, egg, and orange juice until well combined.
4) Pour the wet ingredients into the dry ingredients and stir until just combined. Be careful not to overmix.
5) Pour the batter into the prepared baking dish or divide it evenly between the two ramekins.
6) Sprinkle the chopped pistachios over the top of the batter.
7) Bake in the preheated oven for 25-30 minutes or until a toothpick inserted into the center comes out clean and the top is golden brown.

NUTRITION
Cal 350; Fat 18 g; Carb 45 g;
Protein 6 g; Fiber: 2 g; Sodium: 240 mg

Italian Tiramisu

| Prep time: 20 min | Cook time 4 hours | Serving: 2 |

INGREDIENTS

- *2 cups strong brewed coffee, cooled to room temperature*
- *1/2 cup coffee liqueur (such as Kahlua), optional*
- *3 large egg yolks*
- *1/2 cup granulated sugar*
- *1 cup mascarpone cheese*
- *1 cup heavy cream*
- *1 teaspoon vanilla extract*
- *24-30 ladyfinger cookies (savoiardi)*
- *Unsweetened cocoa powder for dusting*

1) In a shallow dish, combine the cooled brewed coffee and coffee liqueur (if using). Set aside.
2) In a heatproof bowl, whisk together the egg yolks and granulated sugar until pale and thickened.
3) Place the bowl over a pot of simmering water (double boiler) and continue whisking constantly until the mixture is thick and creamy, about 5 minutes. Remove from heat and let it cool slightly.
4) Add the mascarpone cheese to the egg yolk mixture and whisk until smooth and well combined.
5) In a separate bowl, whip the heavy cream and vanilla extract until stiff peaks form.
6) Gently fold the whipped cream into the mascarpone mixture until smooth and creamy.
7) Dip each ladyfinger cookie into the coffee mixture for about 2-3 seconds, making sure not to soak them too much.
8) Arrange a layer of dipped ladyfinger cookies in the bottom of a 9x9-inch (or similar size) dish.
9) Spread half of the mascarpone mixture over the layer of ladyfingers.
10) Repeat with another layer of dipped ladyfingers and remaining mascarpone mixture.

11) Cover and refrigerate the tiramisu for at least 4 hours, or preferably overnight, to allow the flavors to meld and the dessert to set.

12) Before serving, dust the top of the tiramisu with unsweetened cocoa powder using a fine-mesh sieve.

NUTRITION
Cal 380; Fat 22 g; Carb 45 g;
Protein 6 g; Fiber: 2 g; Sodium: 240 mg

Greek Baklava

| Prep time: 20 min | Cook time 50 min | Serving: 4 |

INGREDIENTS

- **For the Filling:**
- *1 pound (about 4 cups) walnuts, finely chopped*
- *1/2 cup granulated sugar*
- *1 teaspoon ground cinnamon*
- **For the Syrup:**
- *1 cup water*
- *1 cup granulated sugar*
- *1/2 cup honey*
- *1 cinnamon stick*
- *1 teaspoon vanilla extract*
- *Zest of 1 lemon*
- **For the Assembly:**
- *1 package (16 ounces) phyllo dough, thawed according to package instructions*
- *1 cup unsalted butter, melted*

1) Preheat your oven to 350°F (175°C). Grease a 9x13-inch baking dish with butter.

2) In a mixing bowl, combine the finely chopped walnuts, granulated sugar, and ground cinnamon. Set aside.

3) Prepare the syrup by combining the water, granulated sugar, honey, cinnamon stick, vanilla extract, and lemon zest in a saucepan. Bring to a boil, then reduce the heat and simmer for 10 minutes. Remove from heat and let it cool while you prepare the baklava.

4) Unwrap the phyllo dough and place it on a clean, dry surface. Cover it with a damp towel to prevent it from drying out.

5) Carefully place one sheet of phyllo dough in the bottom of the prepared baking dish, allowing the edges to hang over the sides. Brush the phyllo sheet with melted butter.

6) Repeat layering phyllo sheets and brushing each sheet with melted butter until you have used about half of the phyllo dough.

7) Spread the walnut filling evenly over the top layer of phyllo in the baking dish.

8) Continue layering the remaining phyllo sheets on top of the walnut filling, brushing each sheet with melted butter.

9) Using a sharp knife, carefully score the top layer of phyllo into diamond or square shapes.

10) Bake the baklava in the preheated oven for 45-50 minutes or until golden brown and crisp.
11) Remove the baklava from the oven and immediately pour the cooled syrup over the hot baklava, making sure to evenly distribute it.
12) Allow the baklava to cool completely in the baking dish before serving, allowing the syrup to soak into the layers.
13) Once cooled, cut the baklava along the scored lines and serve.

NUTRITION
Cal 330; Fat 12 g; Carb 48 g;
Protein 6 g; Fiber: 2 g; Sodium: 240 mg

Cherry Clafoutis

Prep time: 20 min | Cook time: 40 min | Serving: 4

INGREDIENTS

- *1 tablespoon unsalted butter for greasing the baking dish*
- *2 cups fresh cherries, pitted*
- *3 large eggs*
- *1/2 cup granulated sugar*
- *1 cup whole milk*
- *1/2 cup all-purpose flour*
- *1 teaspoon vanilla extract*
- *Pinch of salt*
- *Powdered sugar for dusting*

1) Preheat your oven to 350°F (175°C). Grease a 9-inch pie dish or baking dish with unsalted butter.
2) Arrange the pitted cherries in a single layer in the greased baking dish.
3) In a mixing bowl, whisk together the eggs and granulated sugar until pale and frothy.
4) Gradually add the whole milk, all-purpose flour, vanilla extract, and a pinch of salt to the egg mixture, whisking until smooth and well combined.
5) Pour the batter evenly over the cherries in the baking dish.
6) Bake the clafoutis in the preheated oven for 35-40 minutes or until puffed and golden brown around the edges.
7) Remove the clafoutis from the oven and let it cool for a few minutes.
8) Dust the top of the clafoutis with powdered sugar.
9) Serve the cherry clafoutis warm or at room temperature.

NUTRITION

Cal 250; Fat 10 g; Carb 40 g; Protein 7 g; Fiber: 2 g; Sodium: 90 mg

BREADS, FLATBREADS, PIZZA'S

Greek Salad Pita Pockets

| Prep time: 10 min | Cook time 0 min | Serving: 2 |

INGREDIENTS

- *2 whole-grain pita pockets*
- *1 cup chopped lettuce*
- *1 medium tomato, diced*
- *1/2 cucumber, diced*
- *1/4 red onion, thinly sliced*
- *1/4 cup Kalamata olives, pitted, and sliced*
- *1/4 cup crumbled feta cheese*
- *2 tablespoons olive oil*
- *Salt and black pepper, to taste*

1) Cut the whole-grain pita pockets in half to form pockets.
2) In a mixing bowl, combine the chopped lettuce, diced tomato, diced cucumber, sliced red onion, sliced Kalamata olives, and crumbled feta cheese.
3) Drizzle the olive oil over the salad mixture and season with salt and black pepper to taste. Toss until well combined.
4) Stuff each pita pocket with an equal amount of the Greek salad mixture, pressing down gently to fill the pockets.
5) Serve the Greek Salad Pita Pockets immediately as a delicious and convenient meal option.

NUTRITION
Cal 280; Fat 16 g; Carb 28 g;
Protein 8 g; Fiber: 5 g; Sodium: 560 mg

Mediterranean Flatbread Pizza

Prep time: 15 min	Cook time 12 min	Serving: 2

INGREDIENTS

- 2 whole-grain flatbreads
- 1/2 cup tomato sauce
- 1/2 cup sliced artichoke hearts
- 1/4 cup sliced olives (Kalamata or black)
- 1/4 cup thinly sliced red onion
- 1/4 cup roasted red peppers, sliced
- 1/4 cup crumbled feta cheese
- Olive oil for drizzling (optional)
- Fresh basil leaves for garnish (optional)

1) Preheat the oven to 425°F (220°C).
2) Place the whole-grain flatbreads on a baking sheet lined with parchment paper.
3) Spread 1/4 cup of tomato sauce evenly over each flatbread, leaving a small border around the edges.
4) Arrange the sliced artichoke hearts, olives, red onion, and roasted red peppers on top of the tomato sauce.
5) Sprinkle the crumbled feta cheese over the toppings.
6) Drizzle a little olive oil over the pizzas, if desired, for extra flavor.
7) Transfer the baking sheet to the preheated oven and bake for about 10-12 minutes or until the flatbreads are golden and crispy around the edges, and the cheese is melted and bubbly.
8) Remove the Mediterranean Flatbread Pizzas from the oven and let them cool slightly before slicing.
9) Garnish with fresh basil leaves, if desired, before serving.

NUTRITION
Cal 350; Fat 12 g; Carb 50 g;
Protein 10 g; Fiber: 10 g; Sodium: 800 mg

Veggie Pizza

Prep time: 15 min	Cook time 15 min	Serving: 2

INGREDIENTS

- *1 whole-grain pizza dough (store-bought or homemade)*
- *1/4 cup pesto sauce*
- *1 large tomato, thinly sliced*
- *1/2 bell pepper, thinly sliced*
- *1/4 cup sliced olives (Kalamata or black)*
- *1/4 cup thinly sliced red onion*
- *1/4 cup marinated artichoke hearts, drained, and chopped*
- *1/4 cup crumbled goat cheese*
- *Olive oil for drizzling (optional)*
- *Fresh basil leaves for garnish (optional)*

1) Preheat the oven to the temperature specified on the pizza dough package or recipe (usually around 425°F or 220°C).
2) Roll out the whole-grain pizza dough on a lightly floured surface to your desired thickness and shape. Transfer the rolled-out dough to a baking sheet lined with parchment paper.
3) Spread the pesto sauce evenly over the surface of the pizza dough, leaving a small border around the edges.
4) Arrange the sliced tomato, bell pepper, olives, red onion, and chopped artichoke hearts on top of the pesto sauce.
5) Sprinkle the crumbled goat cheese evenly over the vegetables.
6) Drizzle a little olive oil over the pizza, if desired, for extra flavor.
7) Transfer the baking sheet to the preheated oven and bake for about 12-15 minutes or until the crust is golden and crispy around the edges, and the toppings are heated through.
8) Remove the Mediterranean Veggie Pizza from the oven and let it cool slightly before slicing.
9) Garnish with fresh basil leaves, if desired, before serving.

NUTRITION
Cal 400; Fat 16 g; Carb 50 g; Protein 12 g; Fiber: 8 g; Sodium: 800 mg

Mediterranean Flatbread

| | Prep time: 15 min | | Cook time 10 min | | Serving: 2 |

INGREDIENTS

- *2 cups whole wheat flour*
- *1 teaspoon salt*
- *1 teaspoon baking powder*
- *2 tablespoons extra virgin olive oil*
- *3/4 cup warm water*
- *1 tablespoon honey (optional for a touch of sweetness)*
- *Toppings (optional): chopped olives, sun-dried tomatoes, fresh herbs (such as basil or oregano), crumbled feta cheese, sliced red onion, roasted garlic*

1) Preheat your oven to 450°F (230°C). If you have a pizza stone, place it in the oven to preheat as well. If not, a baking sheet will do.

2) In a large mixing bowl, combine the whole wheat flour, salt, and baking powder. If you're using honey, you can add it to the dry ingredients at this stage.

3) Make a well in the center of the dry ingredients and pour in the olive oil and warm water. Use a wooden spoon or your hands to mix until a dough forms. If the dough is too dry, add a little more water, a tablespoon at a time until it comes together.

4) Transfer the dough to a lightly floured surface and knead it for about 5 minutes or until it becomes smooth and elastic.

5) Divide the dough into 4 equal portions. Take one portion and roll it out into a thin circle, about 1/8 inch thick. Repeat with the remaining portions of dough.

6) If you'd like, you can sprinkle your favorite toppings over the flattened dough circles. Some classic Mediterranean toppings include olives, sun-dried tomatoes, fresh herbs, feta cheese, sliced red onion, and roasted garlic.

7) Carefully transfer the rolled-out flatbreads onto the preheated pizza stone or baking sheet. Bake for 8-10 minutes or until the flatbreads are golden brown and crispy around the edges.

8) Once baked, remove the flatbreads from the oven and let them cool slightly before serving. You can enjoy them warm or at room temperature, plain or with your favorite dips and spreads like hummus, tzatziki, or baba ganoush.

9) Any leftover flatbreads can be stored in an airtight container at room temperature for up to 2 days. You can also freeze them for longer storage; just make sure to wrap them tightly in plastic wrap or foil before freezing.

NUTRITION
Cal 250; Fat 8 g; Carb 35 g;
Protein 8 g; Fiber: 5 g; Sodium: 500 mg

Mediterranean Olive Bread

| Prep time: 10 min | Cook time 30 min | Serving: 2 |

INGREDIENTS

- *2 cups all-purpose flour*
- *1 teaspoon salt*
- *1 teaspoon baking powder*
- *2 tablespoons extra virgin olive oil*
- *3/4 cup warm water*
- *1/2 cup chopped Kalamata olives (or any variety of your choice)*
- *2 tablespoons chopped fresh rosemary*
- *2 cloves garlic, minced*
- *Optional: additional olives for topping, a sprinkle of sea salt*

1) Preheat your oven to 375°F (190°C).
2) In a large mixing bowl, combine the all-purpose flour, salt, and baking powder.
3) Make a well in the center of the dry ingredients and pour in the olive oil and warm water. Mix until a dough forms.
4) Add the chopped olives, chopped rosemary, and minced garlic to the dough. Knead the dough gently until the olives and seasonings are evenly distributed.
5) Transfer the dough to a lightly floured surface and shape it into a round or oval loaf. Optionally, you can press additional olives into the top of the loaf and sprinkle with a little sea salt for extra flavor.
6) Place the shaped loaf on a baking sheet lined with parchment paper. Bake in the preheated oven for 25-30 minutes or until the bread is golden brown and sounds hollow when tapped on the bottom.
7) Remove the olive bread from the oven and let it cool on a wire rack for a few minutes before slicing. Serve warm or at room temperature.

NUTRITION

Cal 200; Fat 8 g; Carb 25 g;
Protein 5 g; Fiber: 2 g; Sodium: 480 mg

Banana Walnut Bread

| Prep time: 15 min | Cook time 30 min | Serving: 2 |

INGREDIENTS

- *1 ripe banana*
- *1/4 cup extra virgin olive oil*
- *1/4 cup honey*
- *1/2 teaspoon vanilla extract*
- *1 egg*
- *1/2 cup whole wheat flour*
- *1/2 teaspoon baking powder*
- *1/4 teaspoon baking soda*
- *1/4 teaspoon salt*
- *1/4 cup chopped walnuts*

1) Preheat your oven to 350°F (175°C). Grease and flour a small loaf pan or line it with parchment paper.

2) In a mixing bowl, mash the ripe banana with a fork until smooth. Add the olive oil, honey, vanilla extract, and egg. Mix well until everything is thoroughly combined.

3) In a separate bowl, whisk together the whole wheat flour, baking powder, baking soda, and salt.

4) Gradually add the dry ingredients to the wet ingredients, stirring until just combined. Be careful not to overmix. Fold in the chopped walnuts.

5) Pour the batter into the prepared loaf pan and spread it out evenly.

6) Place the loaf pan in the preheated oven and bake for 25-30 minutes or until a toothpick inserted into the center comes out clean.

7) Once baked, remove the banana walnut bread from the oven and allow it to cool in the pan for 10 minutes. Then, transfer it to a wire rack to cool completely before slicing.

8) Slice the banana walnut bread and serve it with a drizzle of honey, if desired.

NUTRITION
Cal 350; Fat 16 g; Carb 40 g; Protein 6 g; Fiber: 4 g; Sodium: 250 mg

Mediterranean Pide

Prep time: 20 min | Cook time: 20 min | Serving: 2

INGREDIENTS

- **For the dough:**
- *2 cups all-purpose flour*
- *1 teaspoon active dry yeast*
- *1 teaspoon sugar*
- *1 teaspoon salt*
- *2 tablespoons olive oil*
- *3/4 cup warm water*
- **For the topping:**
- *1 large tomato, thinly sliced*
- *1/2 red onion, thinly sliced*
- *1/2 bell pepper, thinly sliced*
- *1/4 cup sliced black olives*
- *1/4 cup crumbled feta cheese*
- *1 teaspoon dried oregano*
- *1 teaspoon olive oil*
- *Salt and pepper to taste*

1) In a small bowl, mix the warm water, sugar, and yeast. Let it sit for about 5-10 minutes until frothy.

2) In a large mixing bowl, combine the flour and salt. Make a well in the center and pour in the yeast mixture and olive oil.

3) Mix until a dough forms. If the dough is too sticky, add a little more flour. If it's too dry, add a little more water.

4) Knead the dough on a lightly floured surface for about 5-7 minutes until it becomes smooth and elastic.

5) Place the dough in a lightly oiled bowl, cover with a clean kitchen towel, and let it rise in a warm place for about 1 hour or until doubled in size.

Prepare the Topping:

6) Preheat your oven to 425°F (220°C).

7) In a small bowl, toss the tomato slices, red onion slices, bell pepper slices, and black olives with olive oil, dried oregano, salt, and pepper. Set aside.

Shape the Pide:

8) Once the dough has risen, punch it down and divide it into two equal portions.

9) Roll out each portion into an oval shape, about 1/4 inch thick.

10) Transfer the rolled-out dough onto a baking sheet lined with parchment paper.

Assemble and Bake:

11) Arrange the prepared topping mixture evenly over each oval of dough, leaving a border around the edges.
12) Sprinkle the crumbled feta cheese over the topping.
13) Fold the edges of the dough inward to create a border around the topping.
14) Bake in the preheated oven for 15-20 minutes or until the crust is golden brown and crispy.

Serve:

15) Remove the pide from the oven and let it cool slightly before slicing.
16) Serve warm, garnished with fresh herbs if desired.

NUTRITION
Cal 400; Fat 16 g; Carb 55 g;
Protein 12 g; Fiber: 5 g; Sodium: 500 mg

COCKTAIL'S, DRINKS

Mediterranean-Style Mint Lemonade

| Prep time: 10 min | Cook time 0 min | Serving: 4 |

INGREDIENTS

- *2 cups crushed ice*
- *4 cups water*
- *2 large lemons (washed, cut into small pieces, seeds removed)*
- *1 large lemon (for garnish)*
- *1 bunch fresh mint leaves (stems removed, about 25-40 mint leaves, more for later)*
- *1 cup sugar (adjust to your liking)*

1) Wash the lemons thoroughly. Cut two of the lemons into small pieces, removing any seeds. Cut the remaining lemon into thin slices for garnish.
2) Remove the stems from the fresh mint leaves.
3) In a blender, combine the lemon pieces (without seeds), fresh mint leaves, and sugar.
4) Blend until the mixture forms a smooth paste-like consistency.
5) In a large pitcher, add the crushed ice and pour in the water.
6) Add the blended lemon-mint mixture to the pitcher.
7) Stir the mixture well until the sugar is completely dissolved and the flavors are evenly distributed.
8) Add the lemon slices and a few extra mint leaves to the pitcher for garnish.
9) Stir once more before serving to ensure the flavors are well combined.
10) Serve the Mediterranean-style mint lemonade in glasses filled with ice cubes, garnishing each glass with a lemon slice and a sprig of fresh mint.

NUTRITION
Cal 120; Fat 0 g; Carb 30 g; Protein 0 g; Fiber: 2 g; Sodium: 0 mg

Mediterranean Ginger-Rosemary Drink

| Prep time: 10 min | Cook time 0 min | Serving: 4 |

INGREDIENTS

- *4 cups water*
- *1 tablespoon fresh ginger, peeled, and thinly sliced*
- *2-3 sprigs fresh rosemary*
- *1 tablespoon honey (optional, adjust to taste)*
- *Juice of 1 lemon*
- *Ice cubes (optional for serving)*
- *Fresh rosemary sprigs and lemon slices for garnish*

1) In a medium saucepan, bring the water to a gentle boil over medium heat.
2) Add the thinly sliced ginger and rosemary sprigs to the boiling water.
3) Reduce the heat to low and let the mixture simmer for about 10-15 minutes to infuse the flavors.
4) After simmering, remove the saucepan from heat.
5) Stir in honey, if using, until dissolved. Adjust sweetness to your taste preference.
6) Using a fine-mesh sieve or cheesecloth, strain the ginger-rosemary infusion into a heatproof pitcher or container, discarding the ginger and rosemary.
7) Allow the infused liquid to cool to room temperature.
8) Once cooled, stir in the fresh lemon juice. Adjust to taste if necessary.
9) Refrigerate the ginger-rosemary drink until thoroughly chilled, about 1-2 hours.
10) Pour the chilled ginger-rosemary drink into glasses filled with ice cubes, if desired.
11) Garnish each glass with a sprig of fresh rosemary and a slice of lemon.

NUTRITION

Cal 20; Fat 0 g; Carb 5 g;
Protein 0 g; Fiber: 2 g; Sodium: 0 mg

Spiced Pomegranate Ginger Beer Mocktail

Prep time: 10 min | Cook time: 0 min | Serving: 4

INGREDIENTS

- *1 cup pomegranate juice (unsweetened)*
- *1 cup ginger beer (unsweetened or lightly sweetened)*
- *1 tablespoon fresh lime juice*
- *1/2 teaspoon ground cinnamon*
- *1/4 teaspoon ground cloves*
- *Ice cubes*
- *Pomegranate arils and lime slices for garnish*
- *Fresh mint leaves for garnish (optional)*

1) Juice fresh pomegranates to obtain 1 cup of pomegranate juice. Alternatively, you can use store-bought unsweetened pomegranate juice.
2) Juice fresh limes to obtain 1 tablespoon of lime juice.
3) In a mixing bowl or pitcher, combine the pomegranate juice, ginger beer, fresh lime juice, ground cinnamon, and ground cloves. Stir well to combine.
4) Place the mocktail mixture in the refrigerator to chill for about 30 minutes to 1 hour, allowing the flavors to meld.
5) Fill two glasses with ice cubes.
6) Pour the chilled Spiced Pomegranate Ginger Beer Mocktail into the prepared glasses.
7) Garnish each mocktail with a few pomegranate arils, a slice of lime, and a sprig of fresh mint leaves, if desired.

NUTRITION
Cal 80; Fat 0 g; Carb 20 g;
Protein 0 g; Fiber: 1 g; Sodium: 20 mg

Honey Mint Green Iced Tea

| | Prep time: 10 min | | Cook time 0 min | | Serving: 4 |

INGREDIENTS

- *2 cups water*
- *2 green tea bags*
- *1 tablespoon honey (adjust to taste)*
- *1/4 cup fresh mint leaves, plus extra for garnish*
- *Ice cubes*
- *Lemon slices for garnish (optional)*

1) Bring 2 cups of water to a boil in a saucepan or kettle.
2) Once the water reaches a boil, remove it from heat and add the green tea bags.
3) Let the tea bags steep in the hot water for about 3-4 minutes to extract the flavors.
4) After steeping, remove the tea bags from the water.
5) Stir in honey to sweeten the tea, adjusting the amount to your taste preference.
6) Add fresh mint leaves to the hot tea and stir. Let the tea cool down to room temperature.
7) Once the tea has cooled, transfer it to the refrigerator to chill for about 1 hour.
8) Fill two glasses with ice cubes.
9) Pour the chilled Honey Mint Green Tea into the glasses, dividing it evenly.
10) Garnish each glass with a sprig of fresh mint leaves and a slice of lemon, if desired.

NUTRITION

Cal 40; Fat 0 g; Carb 10 g;
Protein 0 g; Fiber: 0 g; Sodium: 0 mg

Carrot Ginger Juice

| Prep time: 10 min | Cook time 0 min | Serving: 2 |

INGREDIENTS

- *4 large carrots, washed, and peeled*
- *1-inch piece of fresh ginger, peeled*
- *1 lemon, peeled (optional for added flavor)*
- *1 tablespoon honey (optional for sweetness)*
- *Ice cubes (optional for serving)*
- *Fresh mint leaves for garnish (optional)*

1) Wash and peel the carrots. Cut them into smaller pieces if needed to fit into your juicer chute.
2) Peel the ginger and cut it into smaller pieces.
3) If using, peel the lemon, making sure to remove any seeds.
4) Using a juicer, juice the carrots, ginger, and lemon (if using) according to the manufacturer's instructions.
5) If you don't have a juicer, you can use a blender. Blend the carrots, ginger, lemon (if using), and a little water until smooth, then strain the mixture through a fine-mesh sieve or cheesecloth to extract the juice.
6) Taste the carrot ginger juice and add honey if desired, adjusting the sweetness to your preference. Stir well to combine.
7) If you prefer your juice cold, you can refrigerate it for about 30 minutes before serving, or add ice cubes directly to the juice.
8) Pour the carrot ginger juice into glasses.
9) If desired, garnish each glass with a sprig of fresh mint leaves for a refreshing touch.

NUTRITION

Cal 80; Fat 0 g; Carb 20 g; Protein 2 g; Fiber: 3 g; Sodium: 100 mg

Greek Yogurt and Berry Smoothie

Prep time: 10 min | Cook time: 0 min | Serving: 2

INGREDIENTS

- *1 cup Greek yogurt (unsweetened)*
- *1/2 cup mixed berries (such as strawberries, blueberries, raspberries)*
- *1 ripe banana*
- *1/2 cup spinach leaves (optional for added nutrition)*
- *1 tablespoon honey (optional for sweetness)*
- *1/2 cup unsweetened almond milk or water*
- *Ice cubes (optional for texture)*
- *Fresh mint leaves for garnish (optional)*

1) If using fresh berries, wash them thoroughly. If using frozen berries, you can thaw them slightly.

2) Peel the ripe banana and break it into smaller chunks.

3) In a blender, combine the Greek yogurt, mixed berries, banana chunks, spinach leaves (if using), honey (if using), and unsweetened almond milk or water.

4) If you prefer a thicker smoothie, you can add a handful of ice cubes to the blender as well.

5) Blend the ingredients on high speed until smooth and creamy. If the consistency is too thick, you can add more almond milk or water to reach your desired consistency.

6) Taste the smoothie and adjust the sweetness by adding more honey if desired. Blend again to combine.

7) Pour the Greek Yogurt and Berry Smoothie into glasses.

8) If desired, garnish each glass with a few fresh mint leaves for a pop of color and extra freshness.

NUTRITION

Cal 200; Fat 6 g; Carb 35 g; Protein 17 g; Fiber: 6 g; Sodium: 100 mg

Mango and Spinach Smoothie

| Prep time: 10 min | Cook time: 0 min | Serving: 1 |

INGREDIENTS

- *1 ripe mango, peeled, and diced*
- *1/2 cup spinach leaves*
- *1/2 cup pineapple chunks*
- *1/2 cup Greek yogurt (unsweetened)*
- *1 tablespoon chia seeds*
- *1/2 cup coconut water (unsweetened)*
- *Ice cubes (optional for texture)*

1) Peel the ripe mango and dice it into chunks.
2) If using fresh pineapple, cut it into chunks. If using canned pineapple, drain the chunks.
3) Wash the spinach leaves thoroughly.
4) In a blender, combine the diced mango, spinach leaves, pineapple chunks, Greek yogurt, chia seeds, and coconut water.
5) If you prefer a thicker smoothie, you can add a handful of ice cubes to the blender as well.
6) Blend the ingredients on high speed until smooth and creamy. If the consistency is too thick, you can add more coconut water to reach your desired consistency.
7) Taste the smoothie and adjust the sweetness or thickness by adding more mango, Greek yogurt, or coconut water as desired.
8) Pour the Mango and Spinach Smoothie into glasses.
9) If desired, garnish each glass with a sprinkle of chia seeds or a slice of fresh mango for decoration.

NUTRITION
Cal 250; Fat 6 g; Carb 45 g;
Protein 12 g; Fiber: 8 g; Sodium: 80 mg

28-DAY MEAL PLAN

	Breakfast	Lunch	Dinner
Monday	Greek Salad Pita Pockets (190)	Beef Kebabs (25) with Mediterranean Tomato Rice (129)	Mediterranean Grilled Chicken (46) with Vegetable Ratatouille (97)
Tuesday	Mediterranean Flatbread Pizza (191)	Greek Style Grilled Lamb Chops (26) with Balsamic Roasted Green Beans (103)	Lemon Garlic Shrimp Skewers (75) with Vegetarian Chili (107)
Wednesday	Veggie Pizza (192)	Lamb Meatballs (28) with Pasta Primavera (133)	Grilled Mediterranean Salmon (73) with Beet and Walnut Salad (166)
Thursday	Mediterranean Pide (196)	Beef and Prunes (32) with Mediterranean Grain Tabbouleh (140)	Duck Breast with Figs and Olives (68) with Mediterranean Gnocchi (106)
Friday	Greek Yogurt and Berry Smoothie (204)	Steak Bowls (36) with Greek Salad Pita Pockets (190)	Mediterranean Turkey Meatloaf (64) with Mediterranean Artichoke Dip (13)
Saturday	Pesto Chicken Quinoa Bowls (141)	Lamb Souvlaki (41) with Greek Couscous Patties (148)	Turkey Wraps (65) with Shrimp and Avocado Salad (163)
Sunday	Turkey Panini (66)	Stuffed Chicken Breast (47) with Vegetable Ratatouille (97)	Turkey Meatball and Orzo Bowl (59) with Turkish Beet Greens (109)

	Breakfast	**Lunch**	**Dinner**
Monday	Winter Squash and Greens Couscous (143)	Balsamic Glazed Chicken Thighs (48) with Fasolakia (113)	Xinomavro Duck with Cornmeal Cream (69) with Stuffed Grape Leaves (Dolmas) (18)
Tuesday	Greek Couscous Patties (148)	Turkey Meatballs (49) with Mediterranean Gnocchi (106)	Mediterranean Baked Cod (74) with Mediterranean Grain Tabbouleh (140)
Wednesday	Warm Salad with Quinoa and Vegetables (157)	Greek Style Lemon Chicken Skewers (50) with Watermelon and Feta Salad (168)	Mediterranean Style Seared Tuna (76) with Horta (Warm Greens Salad) (169)
Thursday	Shrimp and Avocado Salad (163)	Chicken Skillet (54) with Beet and Walnut Salad (166)	Duck Breast with Honey and Spices (71) with Balsamic Roasted Green Beans (103)
Friday	Quinoa with Spinach in Creamy Sauce (155)	Mediterranean Turkey Bowls (56) with Sautéed Kale (104)	Turkey Meatball and Orzo Bowl (59) with Turkish Beet Greens (109)
Saturday	Cauliflower and Farro Salad (176)	Couscous & Chicken Bake (61) with Citrus Avocado Salad (172)	Bifteki (Greek Beef Patties) (43) with Roasted Brussels Sprouts and Pecans (111)
Sunday	Pesto Chicken Quinoa Bowls (141)	Duck Breast with Figs and Olives (68) with Puglia-Style Pasta with Broccoli Sauce (138)	Steak Bowls (36) with Puglia-Style Pasta with Broccoli Sauce (138)

	Breakfast	**Lunch**	**Dinner**
Monday	Bulgur with Eggplant, Zucchini, Tomatoes, and Mushrooms (151)	Spanish-Style Chicken Casserole (52) with Mediterranean Chickpea and Quinoa Salad (164)	Lamb Souvlaki (41) with Couscous with Vegetables and Cheese (154)
Tuesday	Mediterranean Pide (196)	Turkey Meatballs (49) with Mediterranean Gnocchi (106)	Mediterranean Style Seared Tuna (76) with Mediterranean Gnocchi (106)
Wednesday	Greek Yogurt and Berry Smoothie (204)	Duck Breast with Honey and Spices (71) with Mediterranean Couscous Soup (146)	Turkey Wraps (65) with Shrimp and Avocado Salad (163)
Thursday	Mediterranean Grain Tabbouleh (140)	Lemon Garlic Shrimp Skewers (75) with Mediterranean Couscous Skillet (147)	Mediterranean Turkey Meatloaf (64) with Mediterranean Artichoke Dip (13)
Friday	Greek Yogurt Bark with Berries (182)	Mediterranean Baked Cod (74) with Greek Lemon Chicken Soup (Avgolemono) (119)	Chicken Piccata (55) with Orzo with Feta and Marinated Peppers (139)
Saturday	Veggie Pizza (192)	Mediterranean Turkey Bowls (56) with Sautéed Kale (104)	Grilled Mediterranean Salmon (73) with Beet and Walnut Salad (166)
Sunday	Greek Couscous Patties (148)	Chicken Skillet (54) with Beet and Walnut Salad (166)	Grilled Mediterranean Salmon (73) with Beet and Walnut Salad (166)

	Breakfast	**Lunch**	**Dinner**
Monday	Mango and Spinach Smoothie (205)	Stuffed Chicken Breast (47) with Vegetable Ratatouille (97)	Bifteki (Greek Beef Patties) (43) with Roasted Brussels Sprouts and Pecans (111)
Tuesday	Pesto Chicken Quinoa Bowls (141)	Mediterranean Steak Bites (35) with Mediterranean Kale Fried Rice (128)	Lamb Meatballs (28) with Cauliflower and Chickpea Curry (102)
Wednesday	Mediterranean Zoodle Salad (162)	Beef and Prunes (32) with Mediterranean Grain Tabbouleh (140)	Balsamic Glazed Chicken Thighs (48) with Zucchini Noodles with Pesto (94)
Thursday	Spinach Casserole with Two Types of Cheese (156)	Tender Lamb Shanks (29) with Green Bean Stew (105)	Couscous & Chicken Bake (61) with Eggplant Caponata (101).
Friday	Citrus Avocado Salad (172)	Beef Kebabs (25) with Mediterranean Tomato Rice (129)	Chicken Skillet (54) with Green Mediterranean Salad (165)
Saturday	Mediterranean Flatbread (193)	Grilled Lemon Garlic Scallops (78) with Cabbage and Carrot Salad (167)	Turkey Meatballs (49) with Warm Salad with Quinoa and Vegetables (157)
Sunday	Cauliflower and Farro Salad (176)	Shrimp and Vegetable Stir-Fry (80) with Sicilian Salad (171)	Duck Breast with Figs and Olives (68) with Mediterranean Gnocchi (106)

CONCLUSION

Your Journey to a Healthier, Happier Life Starts Now

Congratulations on taking the first step toward a healthier lifestyle with the Mediterranean Diet Cookbook for Beginners. By delving into the diverse and flavorful dishes of the Mediterranean, you have not only adopted a diet that is famed for its numerous health benefits, but you have also found the pleasure of feeding your body and soul at the same time.

Throughout this cookbook, you've learned about 170 delicious recipes that prove healthy eating doesn't mean compromising on taste. From the vibrant salads and hearty mains to the indulgent desserts and refreshing drinks, you've experienced the vast variety that the Mediterranean diet offers.

As you continue your culinary journey, remember that the Mediterranean way of life is more than just the food you eat—it's about enjoying meals with loved ones, savoring each bite, and living in harmony with nature. It's a sustainable approach to health that prioritizes fresh, whole foods and a balanced lifestyle.

No matter what your dietary objective is—weight loss, increased energy, or just a healthier diet—the Mediterranean diet can help you get there without completely neglecting your favorite dishes. The recipes and tips you've explored in this book are valuable tools to help you make informed, delicious choices that support your well-being.

The next chapter of your health journey is in your hands. Continue to experiment with new recipes, share meals with family and friends, and, most importantly, enjoy every step of the way. The Mediterranean diet is a lifelong journey toward better health, and you're well on your way.

Thank you for allowing us to be a part of your journey. Here's to a future filled with tasty meals, excellent health, and the joy that comes from living well and feeling good.

Wishing you health and happiness—now and always.

Printed in Great Britain
by Amazon